Signs

Everett Triplett

2008

For additional copies, order from BookSurge 866-308-6235.
You can order this book from www.Amazon.com

Signs

WORLD WAR THREE IS COMING; A NEW SUPER POWER IS FORMING—IT'S ALL OUR ENEMIES BONDED TOGETHER BY THEIR MUTUAL HATRED FOR US. THEY UNITE AGAINST US BY POOLING TOGETHER THEIR RESOURCES (MAN-POWER, EQUIPMENT, AND FINANCES) TO STOP THE UNITED STATES' DOMINATION OF THE WORLD. GET READY NOW AMERICANS; WE WILL HAVE TO FIGHT ALL OF OUR ENEMIES AT THE SAME TIME. THIS IS THE FINAL CONFLICT; THE END OF THE AGE AS WE KNOW IT, BUT THERE IS COMING A NEW AGE OF LASTING PEACE ON EARTH THAT WILL SURPASS ALL YOUR WILDEST DREAMS.

THE BIBLE PREDICTS:
AMERICA WILL SOON SUFFER A MASSIVE NUCLEAR ATTACK [the Day of the Lord] FOLLOWED BY AN INVASION LEAD BY A RUSSIAN COALITION INCLUDING MUSLIMS [see Ezekiel 38] FROM WHICH WE WILL BARELY RECOVER, ONLY BECAUSE THE LORD WILL RESCUE US [Jeremiah 1:19], WE MUST KEEP ON FIGHTING UNTIL THE LORD SUDDENLY RETURNS WITH RE-INFORCEMENTS [the armies of Heaven, Rev. 19] TO SAVE US FROM TOTAL ANIHILA-TION BY A CHINESE COALITION OF TWO HUN-DRED MILLION [Rev. 9].

WITH THE LORD'S HELP, WE WILL COMPLETELY AND TOTALLY DESTROY ALL OF OUR ENEMIES, AND FULFILL OUR DESTINY AND EMERGE FROM THIS FINAL CONFLICT AS THE CHAMPIONS OF THE NEW WORLD WITH ESTABLISHED PEACE AND CONTIN-

UOUS EXPANDING PROSPERITY FOR A THOUSAND YEARS TO COME.

NOW IS THE TIME TO PREPARE BY BEGINNING AN ACCUMULATION OF ESSENTIAL SUPPLIES ENOUGH FOR MORE THAN A YEAR. UNDERSTANDING OF THIS MESSAGE CAN SAVE YOUR LIFE! YOU NEED TO GET WHILE THE GETTING IS GOOD. WAR IS COMING AND SUDDENLY THE DISTRIBUTION OF ALL KINDS OF SUPPLIES WILL BE INDEFINITELY INTERUPTED.

"WHEN" -THE WEEK—THE MONTH—THE YEAR

CRUCIAL TIMING INFORMATION IS REVEALED IN THE SCRIPTURES. THIS SUDDEN DISASTER (NUCLEAR ATTACK) WILL TAKE PLACE IN THE MIDDLE OF THE NIGHT, DURING THE WEEK OF THE PHASE OF THE NEW MOON AND DURING THE TIME WHEN THE DAYS OF SUNSHINE ARE AT THEIR LONGEST (SUMMER IS NEAR) THE MONTH OF JUNE, AND THE FIELDS OF CROPS ARE NEARLY READY FOR HARVEST. THE SKIES WILL BE FILLED WITH SMOKE FROM BURNING CITIES AND WIND CURRENTS WILL CARRY THE SOOT AND ASH ACROSS THE CROPLANDS RESULTING IN AN ENVIRONMENTAL CONTAMINATION WITH RADIATION OF BOTH SUPPLIES OF FOOD AND SURFACE WATER. THE 390 YEARS SIN ACCUMULATES AND THEN THERE WILL BE 390 DAYS OF PUNISHMENT/SEIGE. A DAY OF PUNUSHMENT IS FOR EACH YEAR OF SIN. ALARMING HISTORIC EVIDENCE INDICATES THE YEAR OF THIS DESTRUCTION COULD BE THIS YEAR.

THE FOLLOWING PAGES CONTAIN THE BIBLICALLY SOUND BASIS FOR THE ABOVE STATEMENTS

This book is dedicated to:
THE C.C.F.F.
CALLED — CHOSEN — FAITHFUL — FOLLOWERS

CHAPTER 1

WASHINGTON, D.C

I penetrated the world's most intense security gauntlet, in an effort to have a one-on-one meeting with President George W. Bush.

To begin with, it's important to point out that I'm just an average American citizen. I've never been in the military, worked in law enforcement, or in any official capacity for the government.

Nevertheless, working as an individual on April 5, 2001, I managed to achieve what many people would not dare attempt, much less accomplish. I gained entrance and walked right into the United States Federal Government's State Department Building in Washington D.C. I walked right past the State Department security guards and high-tech surveillance equipment on the day and at the time that the President of the United States was there engaged in a ceremony with other foreign dignitaries.

People wonder how I achieved the seemingly impossible. Even the world's best trained, highest paid security experts became baffled and bewildered.

They demanded to know how I managed to get inside their building, breaching the highest security in the world. They said that I had made them look like fools. I told them about the important, urgent message I carried for the President.

Well, I promise to reveal compelling, life-changing info about that message. And once you understand those details, they're likely to grip you with fear—changing your life forever.

Before getting to that however, you'll probably want to know the extent I went to reach the President of the United States, heralded as the world's most powerful man.

I'm an average American in my mid-50s, a successful and prosperous building contractor, and a professional real estate sales broker in a small rural Nevada town.

I have discovered such important information so powerful that it affects the lives of every American and the entire world. In fact, your very survival—and the fate of your family—hinges on the urgent details revealed herein.

Determined to get this vital information to as many people as possible, especially powerful politicians, I traveled alone to our nation's capitol. I arrived in Washington, D.C., in the wee hours of the morning.

Driving down the freeway at two o'clock in the morning, the heavy truck traffic that night apparently blocked my view of the sign for the exit I needed to take.

As you'll soon discover, some signs can be extremely important. An exhausted country boy unaccustomed to driving in urban areas, I continued on for what seemed like twenty miles, before realizing I had gone too far. Quickly turning around, upset with myself for not seeing the right sign, I thought to myself, "See how important signs are." Not paying attention has just cost me at lot of time, fuel and badly needed rest. This is an important lesson. I was glad when I finally found my hotel.

After a few hours sleep, the first thing I did that morning was make a beeline to the United States Capitol Building. There, I was anxious to find some of the nation's most powerful leaders, our senators and congressmen.

The moment I entered the Capitol Building, after going through its standard security screening, there was a crowd of people in the hall watching President Bush on TV addressing foreign diplomats at a live televised ceremony with lots of foreign flags.

I casually walked up and asked this guy, "Where is that at?"

He told me it was at the State Department Building on Constitution Avenue, several blocks from the Capitol. Immediately, I returned outside, down the steps out to the street and asked a taxi driver "Can you take me to the State Department?"

A few minutes later, the cab driver pulled over and said, "This is as far as I can go, sir," as he pointed toward the huge building that covers an entire city block, "That's it right there."

Barricades were blocking the street, preventing him from getting any closer. I got out and walked along a sidewalk toward the State Department. I was then stopped by a police officer who told me, "Sir, you cannot pass this point. The President is in here."

"Well, I have come to see him, even if I have to run over the top of you to do it," I said, half serious, but not threateningly. I turned around and walked across the street.

Still, I resolved to try to get into the building. The lives of millions of people hinged on whether I could convey my message to the right people, and so I was dead-set on doing whatever was necessary to gain access into the State Department Building.

At the time, I used a cane to walk, limping as my left leg remained unhealed from a severe break suffered in an industrial accident. In my other hand, I carried a satchel filled with the vital info intended for the President and other politicians.

Driven by determination, guided by instinct and optimism, I walked around the corner and started down a side street. At the same time a woman came walking from across the street, going in the same direction as me. As we merged together on the sidewalk, I could tell she knew where she was going, carrying a full tray of coffee and donuts.

So, I followed immediately behind her, and she walked down the steps into a side entrance of the State Department Building. I held the door open for her, and we entered together. We walked straight across the entry room, ignoring a metal detector to our right and the security guards sitting at their desk.

They obviously knew her, and she probably went in and out daily to get coffee and donuts. Instinctively, I also ignored the security personnel and followed right behind.

Past the metal detector, she put her plastic ID card into a security gate. When it opened, and she went inside, I thought I could also slip through right behind her. But the bar closed, and locked in front of me as she continued on into the building.

Obviously, I found myself unable to proceed forward. So, I turned to the right. And it must have appeared to the security guard—because of my cane and my large satchel—that I was having difficulty passing though the narrow opening and needed help.

He motioned for me to come toward him as he held open a wide gate designed as access for disabled people. With a stern countenance and a serious demeanor I walked by as a man needing to be at an important place and with a nod of appreciation, I said, "Thanks."

It was hard to conceal how ecstatic I felt as I tried not to hurry down the hall and into the heart of the State Department. Now, I knew for sure that God had helped me get in, and I was supposed to be there. After all, they had even held open the gate for me!

Without question, my day had started out great, and it kept getting better. My intentions remained peaceful: to meet with President Bush and talk to him for a few minutes.

Now that I had penetrated the initial layer of security, I had to remain cool, calm, and collected in order to achieve success. I proceeded down the long halls like I knew where I was going. I didn't want to look lost—even though I was—that would surely draw attention to me, and people would ask if I needed help.

As I explored various corridors, I came upon a group of people standing in a hallway intersection outside the cafeteria watching the same ceremony of the President on a monitor. An excited woman among them said, "My hand just shook the hand of the President. I'm never going to wash it again."

I held out my hand to her and asked, "Can I shake the hand of the hand that shook the President's?"

Without hesitation, the woman shook my hand. I thought, "If she could get that close, so could I." Then, I asked them, "Where is that ceremony at?"

Someone said, "It's on the Eighth Floor in the Franklin Room." So I immediately set out to find an elevator, with a serious and stern countenance—like an official on a grave mission.

Since I didn't know how long the ceremony would last, time remained of the essence. The first elevator I found only went to the seventh floor.

Arriving there, I stepped out into an area crowded with people. But there was no sign of the President. I asked, "How do you get to the Eighth Floor?" Several people pointed to another elevator, telling me, "That's the one that goes there."

As I walked over to that elevator, three Secret Service agents stood in front of it. I boldly tried to step past them.

"This elevator is closed," one of them said.

"Oh," I said, and without making an issue of it, I turned and walked down the hallway. Although somewhat stymied, I continued down the hallway with unwavering determination. Then I spotted a freight elevator, and I entered it at the same time as a janitor. He asked me, "What floor, sir?"

"I want to go to the eighth floor."

"Well, this elevator doesn't go there, and the only elevator to the eight floor is temporarily closed," he said. "But I can show you a door to the stairway that goes there."

"Okay."

A few minutes later as we stepped out on the first floor, he said, "There's the door," pointing to the stairway. He went on his way, and I began climbing the eight flights of stairs.

I remained in good shape for a forty-eight-year-old man. In spite of the pain in my half-healed broken leg, with determination I finally reached the eighth floor.

Just as I opened the stairwell door to that floor where no one from the public was supposed to venture, I startled a security guard standing there.

"Excuse me," I said, continuing right past him like I was headed somewhere important.

"Just a minute, sir," he said. "Do you work here?"

"Well, waduya think?" I responded in a tone of disgust, trying to imply would I be here if they weren't paying me? Like he was asking a ridiculous question, as I continued walking. I did not want to lie to him. But my answer failed to satisfy the guard, and he began to follow me "Well just exactly where do you work?" he asked.

I stopped and confessed, "I'm a visitor," I responded truthfully.

"Hey, you don't have an ID badge!" the guard suddenly noticed.

By this point I had been in the building nearly one hour, and until now no one had noticed that I even lacked such a badge—required to be worn by virtually every person in the entire building—employees and visitors alike.

"I don't have one," I told the guard.

"Well, you have to have one. Come with me, and I'll take you to the front desk and show you where to get one."

I was co-operative and grateful, but then he realized he was supposed to be at his post so he asked another guard to accompany me downstairs to the lobby. At the front desk, the receptionist who issues visitor ID passes asked me, "Who are you here to see?"

"Colin Powell."

I knew Powell, Secretary of State at the time, would be an excellent initial contact. He enjoyed full access to communication with the President.

The receptionist asked me if I had an appointment. When I told her "no," she directed me to the in-house phone in the lobby and gave me the extension number to Powell's office.

I spoke to Powell's personal secretary, who asked me to hold the line. While on hold, I noticed a man standing behind me, and then a few more gathered around me. At first I figured they were waiting to use the phone, but then it became clear they wanted to talk to me.

"We'd like to have a word with you, sir," one of the men said. "Could you come with us for a minute?"

"Certainly," I said, fully cooperative.

INTEROGATIONS

They escorted me to a nearby conference room, and asked if I would like something to drink—coffee or soda.

"We're interested in what you're doing here, and what your purpose is." one of them said. "You've successfully breached our security by entering our building without proper authorization."

I cooperated completely and honestly. I had nothing to hide and I wanted as many people as possible to learn of plans to destroy the United States.

"We want to know how you got into our building. You've made us look like fools," the obviously distressed official said. "We're a highly trained security force, the best in the world, and you've violated our security. This building is among the most secure buildings in the whole world. No one is supposed to be able to penetrate it."

I said, "The Lord helped me get in because he wants me to have your attention."

"Well, you've certainly got it," the chief security officer said.

Then I began to explain with compelling logic the reason for my being there.

The officers seemed perplexed, stunned by the information I provided along with irrefutable facts that you'll learn much more about in this book.

1 SURPRISE NUCLEAR ATTACK: World War III will begin with an alliance of our enemies launching a surprise nuclear attack on multiple cities in the United States and England.

2 DEATHS: Two thirds of the people who live on one-fourth of the earth will die. And a retaliation results with one-third of the earth's population being annihilated.

3 TARGETED CITIES: Our enemies will hit many of the USA's largest cities with nuclear bombs, particularly including metropolitan areas along the Pacific Coast and the Atlantic Coast.

4 TIMING: This nuclear attack will come under cover of darkness in the middle of the night, during the phase of the new moon; when summer is near; it is at the door. Being before harvest and resulting in fallout contaminating the crops across the land, and thus this attack will cause intense famine.

5 DIRECTION OF ATTACKS: The alliance of attackers will come from—or out of their place in the north.

6 NUCLEAR FALLOUT: One-third of our people will die from radiation sickness and famine in cities, and another one-third will perish in the country by the sword like as in an invasion of enemies. Plus violence will erupt among our own people such as looting, pillaging, plundering, chaos, lawlessness, and anarchy.

7 TIME TO PLAN: Those who follow these instructions will increase their chances of survival.

8 ULTIMATE VICTORY: In the end, we'll totally annihilate and completely destroy all of our enemies, once and for all—ushering in the coming new era of peace on earth for a thousand years, the New Millennium.

CHAPTER 2

GET READY NOW!!

After the attack on America on 9-11-2001, everyone could plainly see that the world is facing escalated turmoil. Hurricane after hurricane destroyed the Gulf Coast refineries and broke levees in New Orleans. Also, a tsunami that killed more than 230,000 people, and people worldwide also were hit by extreme floods, millions of people were suddenly left without power when the national power grid cascaded from one sector to another; unprecedented wild fires ravaged rangelands, killing thousands of livestock; and the worst season of multiple tornadoes ever recorded ripped through multiple communities, destroying lives and leaving behind a wake of unprecedented devastation. We are a nation at war, and the war on terrorism is spreading from the overthrow of the Taliban in Afghanistan to the overthrow of Saddam in Iraq—the Al-Qaeda Terrorist Network that still threatens us.

Starting with the 1999 U.S. led NATO bombing of Yugoslavia to the fact that Osama Bin Laden is still at large and evading justice, all give cause for concern about where this world is headed. An end is coming! But it is not the end of the world, just the end of the world, as we know it. It is this age that is coming to an end. All these major historic calamities are like contractions from birth pains. When the birth pain process has begun and there is no stopping it. What is being born? It is the birthing of a glorious new age, a vast improvement to the way things are today.

Worsening matters, the longstanding ABM treaty between Russia and the United States has been broken. When President Bush approached Russian leader, Valadimir Putin to mutually consent to abandon the treaty, Putin told him that the treaty was the hinge pin on which world peace and stability revolve. That treaty banned the deployment of a missile defense system by the United States. They don't trust us. Previous Russian leader Mikhail Gorbachev said in the past said they can't let us build one, because once we have a missile defense system in place we could use it as a shield from which to launch a pre-emptive strike. We have enjoyed peace in our lifetime based on mutually assured destruction. But now because we have been attacked and need to protect the country, the current administration has made it a top priority. When Mr. Putin was informed that President Bush was withdrawing from the treaty, he said with a solemn, stern countenance, "Mr. Bush makes a mistake."

China has vowed to keep Taiwan from becoming independent, even if it means nuclear war with the United States. This is a major unresolved issue that is not going to go away. Nuclear weapon proliferation by hostile nations like North Korea and Iran make for an uncertain future world.

On December 7, 1941 the world witnessed how war begins. Japan had prepared and planned an attack with all their planes and all their ships and all their men to strike the United States with all the destructive force they could muster. That is the rudimentary fundamental of war: to assemble the biggest club with which to clobber your enemy. Then you watch and wait for the right opportunity to strike. Japan must have observed the United States becoming militarily committed in Europe giving them the opportunity to strike while we were at a reduced military capacity When it comes to war, you cannot pussyfoot around. It is a different world we live in today than in 1941. Today the most destructive capability exists in nuclear weapons, and the plans to use them against us are in the making. We are in a similar reduced capacity now because of the war on terror.

Basically, world events all come down to this: There is justifiable concern for being prepared for the worst-case scenario—a massive nuclear attack on multiple cities simultaneously by an alliance formed of nations who are opposed to the United States. This attack is coming in the middle of a dark night of a new moon before the harvest contaminating the nation's food supply and surface water. Following the bombing will come an invasion by large and mighty army, the likes of which has never been before and will never be again—Book of Joel, Chapter 2.

This is the time of the end-spoken of in the Bible over 2,000 years ago. It's time to be prepared, for deal with it we must. Surviving it is our obligation to future generations. Recovering and retaliating is our destiny.

We will execute vengeance on the nations that attempted to annihilate us, and we will secure the peace for future generations in a new world without anymore war.

YOU NEED TO UNDERSTAND THIS MESSAGE

I did not speak with President Bush or then-Secretary of State Colin Powell that day. But they and other top U.S. officials still must heed these urgent details.

"They'll be informed," the chief of security promised me.

Alarmingly, I've learned there can be no way for us to prevent the attacks because our destiny has been set, and things are in motion that no man can change.

If U.S. officials take heed to the information from this document you're reading now, they could and should step up efforts to teach U.S. citizens to be prepared to deal with a nuclear attack and save themselves.

It is extremely fortunate to have this timely information and understanding. It is because of the Lord's mercy and loving kindness even now that you are being informed. It is not God's will, but many will be totally blindsided by this coming sudden destruction because they are too busy with the cares of life to take time to listen. Now you can see the warning signs and follow instructions to position yourself and your family for survival.

In this book you're reading now, I will reveal the scriptures that provide God's plan for establishing lasting world peace.

But will you be willing to pay the price for this ultimate gift that we can bestow upon future generations? It says they loved not their lives to the death. That is the depth of the commitment of the radical Muslims. Unless we are willing to be committed to the freedom we hold dear to a greater degree than our enemies, how can we prevail?

The fact is that the Lord has provoked and stirred up our enemies against us. Unless you heed the warnings listed here, you could be killed suddenly in the middle of the night.

Top American officials openly admit that an attack on us is imminent. Vice President Dick Cheney has conceded that it's not a matter of if an attack is coming, but only a question of when. The entire thrust of this message is all about "WHEN."

CHAPTER 3

GREATEST RIDDLE OF ALL TIME REVEALED!

The Bible tells of a sudden disaster that comes upon a people who are busy buying and selling, building and planting, and giving in marriage. It is called, "The Day of the Lord." We are told that no one knows the day or the hour. That does leave open the potential to know the week and the month and the year. I have discovered that God does reveal it in the scriptures in simple words. Here in this message you will clearly see the answer to the Greatest Riddle of All Time. When will the End come? It is in the Bible, down to the week, the month, and the formula for adding up to the year.

With relentless determination, our enemies are busy planning a sudden surprise attack that will make Pearl Harbor and 911 pale in comparison, except it will be with our complete and total destruction in mind. Ultimately, though, the Lord says in Jeremiah repeatedly "...do not destroy them completely." They will fight against you but they will not overcome you for I am with you and will rescue you, Jeremiah 1:19.

Of course, for the most part we in the United States perceive ourselves as a peaceful, loving people focused on doing good. Yet much of the world views us in a far different light, partly due to misinformation spread by opposing government leaders.

Herein lays the urgent and relentless need to remain vigilant in protecting ourselves. As the world's sole remaining superpower, we can and must remain forthright in learning the plans and efforts of those who seek to do us harm.

THIS IS URGENT INFORMATION

I have discovered intricate details of the coming nuclear attack within the Holy Bible. Even people who've never read it before become amazed, stunned and concerned when I explain to them the following specific details.

Amazingly, although written well over 2,000 years ago, specific sections of the Bible—penned by the inspired scribes of hundreds and even thousands of years apart—corroborate many similar irrefutable references to today's modern society. These parallel to current times, issues, and locations. There are compelling details and descriptions of this upcoming attack on the United States.

Throughout my adult life, I've considered myself a faithful servant of the Lord. God has given me a gift of insight, simply to believe and explain exactly what his word says.

You will see, the Lord has appointed me to be a watchman as described in Ezekiel 3. In the Bible's Book of Amos 3:7 we're told "surely the sovereign Lord God does nothing without revealing his plan to his servants." I boldly declare before you that He has revealed His plan to me. And He is ready to do what He said He would do from the beginning of the foundation of the world, and there will be no more delay!

TO UNDERSTAND IS TO PREPARE

The Bible's Book of Ezekiel says that the watchman is sent to a stubborn and obstinate people who will not listen to you, because they are not listening to me, but I will make you even more stubborn and obstinate than they are.

Although the First Amendment guarantees freedom of religion and freedom of speech, church leaders became upset about the compelling message of warning that I continually give today. Some considered me disruptive, provoking too much fear. Isaiah 31 says, "to understand this message is to be filled with sheer terror." To understand is to prepare. In days to come you will understand it clearly."-Jeremiah 23:20.

I don't know why the Lord picked me as a watchman, but I'm his servant. I am determined to do whatever His will is and to do whatever it takes to spread this warning.

As the scriptures say the people will be caught up in the cares of this life, and destruction will come upon them unawares. Many people will choose to ignore these warnings; for they are too busy just trying to make a living. Others are lazy-minded, locked in their boring everyday routines while surrounded by their comfort zone—oblivious to the signs of the time. Failure to pay attention to the signs can cost you your life. You don't want to be one of those people today.

Instead perhaps you've been getting an increased sense that something treacherous is upon us—the makings of a cataclysmic event.

The news reports continue to support the evidence that our enemies are rallying together. Their mutual hatred is bonding them into a military alliance. Meantime, much of our society continues to party on and remains ensconced in complete denial as if nothing serious can occur.

THE GREATEST RIDDLE OF ALL TIME

I do feel so all alone with the burden of knowing what is about to happen. I constantly feel the urgent need to warn my fellow countrymen as if I don't succeed, no one else will. Millions of lives are at stake. For who understands the timing of the Day of the Lord? It is the greatest riddle of all time, and God has revealed the answer of it to me. I don't know of anybody else who sees in the scriptures all that I see, foretelling—most importantly—when these things will happen.

SIGNS FROM GOD

Beginning in 1999, strange events suddenly took place in my life that can only be explained as God showing me many important signs pointing to the specific details of what is going to happen soon in our time and bringing about the end of this age.

Here's a brief summary of some of them:

1 ACCIDENT: I suddenly suffered severe injuries in an accident at work. My left arm and my left leg were both shattered when I slipped and fell from a roof. Upon arriving home after orthopedic surgery, in I asked for a Bible and immediately open it to a verse that says: "As for you lie down on your left side."

2 RECOVERY: The suffering and recovery process from these injuries also reflected these scriptures, and I was allowed time to read and begin to understand the prophecies of what is to come.

3 SECOND INJURY: I suffered another injury in a second accident, once again similar to specifics described in the Bible.

4 TELEVISION: Television programs came on repeatedly—depicting the same descriptions of what it will be like—just as I had just finished reading about them in Bible scriptures.

5 SCRIPTURES: I awoke in the middle of the night, and I read a portion of key scripture and recognized it as an example of 1) how this end-time period will unfold, 2) the sequence of events that are to take place, and 3) the total annihilation of all our enemies. The very next morning at an ongoing outdoor Bible reading meeting I was surprisingly asked to publicly read that exact same scripture over a microphone in the front lawn of the U. S. Capitol.

6 THE BIBLE: I would randomly open my Bible to read and instantly recognize and understand direct references about end-time prophecies—some linked as signs indicating the significance of my injuries.

7 PRAYER: Two ladies I had never seen before and have never seen again approached me at the end of the Stockton, California Promise Keeper's meeting and asked me if I needed prayer. "Sure," I said. And as they prayed over me, the one lady said "The Lord has called you to be a WATCHMAN—you have an important job to do and you are to be faithful to do it and not to neglect it!" I consider myself a tough guy and when my bones were shattered I didn't whimper and no tears ran down my face, but when those words were spoken over me I cried, for I already

knew it was true, and I felt overwhelmed because the Lord was using them to confirm it to me.

Well, many people are amazed when I admit that in the late 1960s and early 1970s I was a rebellious hippie. I dropped out of high school to party, play around, and smoke marijuana during the era of free love, peace, and "live and let be."

But I soon discovered that sinful lifestyle reaps death and depression. Just like the Bible says the wages of sin is death. Right after my late teens, I gave my heart to Jesus, and my life has never been the same. I also realized the importance of hard work, family, and an unfailing commitment to God.

At this point, it's essential to emphasize that this message isn't intended to be about me. Instead, it's about you and your family and how to prepare to survive with specific detailed instructions.

As I've already mentioned, today I'm a fairly successful businessman as a general engineering contractor and real estate broker. Like everyone else, I have limited personal resources, but I am using my money to bring this message to you. I'm seeking no personal financial reward by distributing it. I seek a greater reward from my heavenly Father.

THE UNITED STATES IS THE TARGET

Because we're the most powerful nation on earth and the world's last remaining superpower, the book of Jeremiah 5:27 describes us by saying they have become rich and powerful. And Isaiah 18 says, "Go swift messengers to a people of smooth-skinned people feared far and wide, with strange speech and whose land is divided by many rivers."

This nation more than any other, has many major rivers ranging from the Mississippi, Ohio, Missouri, Columbia, Colorado, and the Snake River dividing our land on multiple state boundaries. Other rivers include the Red River dividing Texas from Oklahoma, the Savannah River, the Delaware, and there are more I could name that define in part state boundaries in our vast and great land. And as Isaiah foretold, the people would have strange speech. English most definitely would have sounded strange to Isaiah.

It is obvious to me that large portions of the book of Jeremiah are prophetically applicable to the United States.

Through research and observation, I have discovered that when certain words, phrases or actions are mentioned in the Bible—written over thousands of years ago—they refer to this same unique end-time event. Some of these include:

1 THE FOUR JUDGMENTS: Wherever you find the four judgments that are mentioned in Ezekiel 14:21 you can recognize it is on the subject of this unique, one-of-a-kind end-time of distress and trouble.

a. SWORD
b. FAMINE
c. PLAGUE
d. WILD BEASTS.

2 NORTH REFERENCES: When the word "north" is mentioned with a disaster or an army, it equates to the places from which the attackers will come from on the day of the Lord. Because Ezekiel 5:9 says it will only happen once and never again, so you know it is the same event. Ezekiel 7:5 in the NASV refers to the end is coming and a *UNIQUE DISASTER it is coming. It is the fire cloud of Ezekiel 1:4...coming out of the north...*

3 BIRTH PAINS: When various scriptures mention birth pains or labor pains, they give a direct reference likening it to the end-time of distress that begins with the day of the Lord and culminates in the birthing of new life, the coming new age of peace on earth.

4 SODOM AND GOMORRAH: Whenever these cities get mentioned, the context refers to the time of the end because they are an example of what is going to happen according to 2 Peter 2, they were condemned and burned to ashes because of their wickedness. So that is exactly what is going to happen is that cities will be burned like them.

5 SCROLL: From early scriptures through Revelation, men who created the Bible through inspiration of God referred to the end-time when they talked about a scroll; or eating a scroll; or a hand reached out to them, and it had a scroll in it with writing on both sides. The contents of the scrolls in different books consistently describe similar judgments lending evidence they are the same. It is as if the Lord made copies of a scroll and passed them out to the men who then wrote down in their words what the scroll says.

6 FIRE: Numerous portions of scriptures foretell of burning; judgment by fire; cities burning with fire; smoke filled skies darkening the sun; The elements melting from the fervent heat; people burned to lime.

7 SIGNS: If the scriptures contain the word sign I have found those portions of scripture to be of the content about signs that pertain to these end times.

I AM AN EXAMPLE

I now know that what has happened to me is an example of what's coming to America. In the midst of carrying on a hectic schedule of business affairs, running a real estate office, and general contracting jobs, I found myself suddenly stopped cold turkey. A sudden disaster is upon me. The Day of the Lord is a sudden destruction that comes upon a people who are busy buying, and selling, and building, and planting.

In April 1999, my foot slipped on the edge of a shiny new metal roof we had just installed. I hit the concrete below with extended arms and legs on my left side. I lay there looking at the tip of a bone fragment protruding out of the skin on my left wrist.

I tried to get up. My left ankle wasn't responding. I went in an instant from a macho hard working man's man to a man lying there saying, "Help, I've fallen, and I can't get up."

Deuteronomy 32:28 says, *"They are a nation without sense, there is no discernment in them. If only they were wise and would understand this and discern what their end will be!"* A few verses later, it says, *"In due time their foot will slip; their day of disaster is near and their doom rushes upon them."* Suddenly my foot slipped!

"Say to them, I am a sign to you, As I have done, so it will be done to them." Ezekiel 12:11, in obedience to this scripture I say to you, that I am a sign to you.

I was helped up by a co-worker, and with his assistance I hopped to my truck on my good leg. My left shoe swung back and forth at the end of my leg, and I dripped a trail of blood down the sidewalk from the chip of bone sticking out of my shattered wrist. We arrived at the small town emergency room about noon and after a lengthy exanimation, they made arrangements for me to be taken by ambulance into Reno. I am certain that ambulance was in bad need of shocks, for I felt every bump in the road with excruciating pain of sharp bone fragments jolting around for over an hour.

Upon my arrival at the Reno hospital's emergency room at about four thirty I was told I'd have to wait until they could get to me. I sat there until eleven o'clock waiting for what seemed like forever. Finally my turn came and I under went orthopedic surgery. I awakened from anesthesia, and the first sight I saw was my arm swollen—double its normal size. I had been impaled with steel bolts that were protruding out and connected together with rods and clamps.

Then, my eyes followed down my leg where a bar had been run clear through my heel. Connections on both ends of it reached bars that connected to two bolts screwed into my shinbone. The first thing I said to my wife was, "If you don't get me out of this place these hospital bills will bankrupt us."

Reluctantly, she consented because we were not insured, as I was self-employed.

Immediately after I arrived home from the hospital, my wife brought me medicine and the remote to the TV. She propped me up with several pillows trying to make me as comfortable as possible. She asked, "Is there anything else I can get for you?"

"See if you can find me a Bible," I said. "I don't' know why this has happened to me. But if the Lord wanted to get my attention, he certainly did." She returned from the other room with a brand new American Standard Version still in its box. When I opened it near the middle, my eyes immediately gazed at a verse in Ezekiel 4:4

It said:

"As for you, lie down on your left side."

THIS IS A SIGN

There I was, lying down; I was unable to get up. Both my left arm and my left leg were shattered, swollen double their normal size and impaled with $10,000 worth of stainless steel orthopedic hardware.

Totally convinced that the Lord was trying to tell me something, I became determined to see what it was talking about. After all, I had been reading my Bible for more than twenty years, and I could never remember having seen that verse before. I then read the preceding context trying to see what it meant. It says, *"This is a sign to the house of Israel."* I now know that when the scriptures make any reference to a sign that it is about these end times. I thought why does the Lord tell us this is a sign. We have signs all around us. Some are octagon shaped and painted red with four white letters STOP on them. I began to understand. See what happens if you ignore those signs, it could be the last thing you do. It could cost you your life. When the Lord says "This is a sign" we had better pay attention.

The chapter begins with, *"Son of man get yourself a brick, build a siege wall, put up a ramp and then get an iron plate and set it up as an iron wall and put it between you and the city.* As a builder, I like to know why something is being built.

From that point, I began to read until I got to a verse in the next chapter [5:9] that says, *"Because of your abominations, I will do among you what I've never done before, the like of which I will never do again."*

I thought about that verse, "What can this be that God is coming to do. It has never been done before; and it will never be done again" With an inquiring mind that wants to know, I read on till I got to Chapter 7:5, and it says, *"A disaster, a unique disaster, behold it is coming. An end is coming."* The end has come!

So there is a "UNIQUE DISASTER" coming and because I have an inquiring mind, I wanted to understand just what is going to happen?

CHAPTER 4

THE LORD'S MESSAGE

It became clear to me that the Book of Ezekiel is similar to the Book of Revelations in that it talks about this time of the end. At that time I was puzzled about what this coming unique end time disaster could possibly be. It has never been done before and will never be done again So I decided that I needed to start at the beginning of the Book of Ezekiel.

I had been home three days, and it was about mid-morning. I had just begun to read in Chapter 1, Verse 4, where it says Ezekiel looked and he saw coming out of the north a great cloud of fire enfolding itself—surrounded by brilliant light.

Right as I was thinking, "Can this be a description of a nuclear mushroom cloud?" there was a knock at the front door. I couldn't get up and answer it, my leg was broken, and so I just hollered: "Come on in!"

An eighty-year-old friend of mine named Doc came in and sat down. He said, "I heard you were hurt, so I thought I'd stop by and check on you to see how you're doing."

I'm now convinced the Lord sent him, because after visiting a few minutes, I told him about the verse in Ezekiel 1:4 that I had just been reading right when he knocked on the door. I asked Doc, "Do you think the Ezekiel could be talking about a mushroom cloud of a nuclear bomb?"

He began to tell me how he had been in the South Pacific on a ship in the Navy after World War II. They were conducting atomic bomb tests. He said, "I've seen those bombs go off." The order was given, "You must tightly close your eyes and cover your eyes with your forearm." Doc said that when the bomb detonated, every man on the ship saw the bones in his forearm through his tightly closed eyes. Ezekiel says that he saw an immense fire cloud, infolding itself, surrounded by a brilliant light. Now that definitely qualifies as brilliant light.

It has since occurred to me that not many men like Doc are around, who have personally witnessed nuclear bomb tests. Those kind of men are few and far between. I'm thinking the odds are greater than at least one in ten thousand people who can say they were there and saw a nuclear bomb explode, yet at the exact same minute I am reading about it, I have a man like that knock on my front door and he comes in and explains to me what it is like. Truly the Lord sent him to me and my understanding grows.

Now I wanted to see if there were other scriptures that supported this scenario. I became determined to carefully review the Bible for further evidence in support of a nuclear holocaust. You will be astonished at the amount of scriptures I am going to reveal.

After all, I was held hostage by my broken body, and I had nowhere to go and nothing else to do but immerse myself in the scriptures. I became hungry for God's word. Things I had read before now had new meaning. This was totally new for me.

NUCLEAR BOMBS DROPPED BY JETS

What Ezekiel, Chapter 1 clearly warns of, does come out of the north—a windstorm and an immense cloud with flashing lightning. With what seems to be the description of a mushroom cloud followed by these details; it is not difficult for one to perceive them to be jet aircraft.

Ezekiel says he sees what appears to be the likeness of four living creatures that come out of the midst of the fire cloud. One biblical version says they gleam like burnished bronze (an indication they are made of metal.) They each one have four faces, and each one has four wings, with two that touch one another. An observation of four modern jet aircraft flying in tight formation can appear to have their wings touching. They are often in groups of four together—even while moving straight forward without turning as a jet in flight.

Ezekiel said their legs are straight and they have feet like calves feet. I have heard the expression used about something being as crooked as a dog's hind leg. I thought the dog's hind leg is not particularly more crooked than other animal's hind legs but Ezekiel felt it was important to tell us that these legs are straight possibly because he had never seen anything with straight legs before. A jet can have two tires at the end of the straight leg as landing gear. The silhouette would form two ovals giving the appearance like a divided hoof.

And Ezekiel never says that they are living creatures. They only have the likeness of living creatures. It is the same as a bowl of wax fruit sitting on a table that has a likeness to fruit, but you cannot eat it. Then he specifies that these creatures have four faces, the face of a man, the face of a lion, the face of an ox, and the face of an eagle. But there is no mention of four heads.

My first impulse was to think of a face as part of a head, but the word "face" has other meanings, as in face of the earth or face of a cliff. So how else can we define what your face is?

It is your single most conspicuous and unique and identifiable characteristic. It is the single most obvious and prominent feature that identifies you as unique from others. You may have had an experience like me of seeing someone from a distance who you thought was an old friend, but when you approached them an saw their face you then realized they weren't who you thought.

1 Man stands out from all other of God's creation as the most Intelligent

2 The Lion is known as the ultimate ferocious Predator

3 The ox is known for its Power

4 The eagle is the superior Master of the Sky

Jet aircraft would appear to a man from ancient times to be Intelligent, Predatory, Powerful, and Masters of the Sky, all at the same time.

Try to understand what it would be like to live in the time of Ezekiel and to then be shown future events as they are taking place in today's modern time. After you are shown these things you are then instructed to go and write down what you saw. Ezekiel was a rare man in his day in that few men were educated to read and write; but he was intelligent and educated. Any man from that time period would be hard pressed to do a better job of describing modern jets using the existing vocabulary of that time.

Should we find it difficult to believe that Ezekiel is describing four jets if this is a mushroom cloud of a nuclear bomb that has been delivered and dropped by the jets that are flying or coming out of the midst of the fire? Are not today's enemy aircraft capable of flying low enough to be undetected by modern radar?

I see the evidence in Ezekiel's writing that he witnessed these future events as they were happening. I suspect that time has no barriers for God. He can freely go forward into the future and back into the past. This would lend credibility to the concept of time travel. Insight of other scriptures also reveals details of modern warfare and weapons of mass destruction; an indication that the future has already taken place and it has been written down exactly like it will happen.

SIEGE WALL — BOMB SHELTER

In the section where it says to lie on your left side are instructions to put a barrier between yourself and the city: "Get yourself a brick, and build a siege wall." Then, it says to set up an iron plate like steel-reinforced masonry wall which must be strategically placed between you and the metropolitan area. This design would effectively deflect the 400-mile-per-hour winds produced by a nuclear blast, protecting you as you lay on your left side behind the wall. Just like in modern building codes today, iron is used in reinforcement of masonry block and is necessary for withstanding seismic activity.

We're instructed to gather enough food and other resources to survive 390 days, over one year, long enough for most of the radiation to dissipate and get to harvest time the next year.

Also, homes constructed with brick or concrete exteriors, especially those reinforced with iron, are more likely to remain standing than wood structures outside ground-zero areas.

Today, there's a misconception that a nuclear blast produces radiation that will make an area uninhabitable for thousands of years.

Yet we know from Hiroshima and Nagasaki, (the Japanese communities obliterated by nuclear blasts at the end of World War II) that such communities can be rebuilt over time. Those regions now have thriving populations.

SHOULD YOU BUILD A SIEGE WALL?

Build a siege wall if you're near the outskirts of a major metropolitan area. But build it far enough away that the actual blast is unlikely to cause death. People living or staying overnight in major cities—at or very close to ground zero areas—would not survive the explosions even if they had built siege walls there. It is imperative that you avoid staying at the largest cities that are likely high profile target areas, particularly during the time that these important scriptures reveal.

Instead, you should live or work in mountain or countryside areas where there is a much greater chance of long-term survival. According to Ezekiel 7 all who survive and escape will be in the mountains, but they have baldness on their heads. A well known side effect of radiation exposure is a person's hair all falls out. Supporting evidence continued to accumulate.

ANOTHER SIGN

At the time of my accident, I had planned to build and lease out a new office building to a cable TV company. I had even signed a notice of intent to do that. But my injury and the recovery process made this impossible. Prayerfully, I opened my Bible seeking direction about this existing commitment. My eyes focused on Jeremiah 45:5, which asks *"Should you then seek great things for yourself? Seek them not, for I will bring disaster on all people declares the Lord. But wherever you go, I will let you escape with your life."* The Lord certainly had my attention, just like I'm trying to get yours now.

This end-time disaster is coming, and it requires us to stop seeking great things for ourselves and change our plans to make way for the coming of the Lord. His plans supersede ours and Amos 3:6 says *"Surely the sovereign Lord God does nothing without first revealing His plans to His servants the prophets."*

Up to this point in life, I had been seeking to become wealthy and to have commercial properties full of tenants generating monthly cash flows for me and my family. I telephoned my client, and I told them what had happened to me. And we mutually agreed to indefinitely postpone our plans.

ANALYZE EVERY WORD OF SCRIPTURE

The verse I turned to upon immediately arriving home from the hospital with a shattered left arm and a shattered left leg, says: *"As for you, lay down on your left side."* I readily perceived that the Lord was trying to tell me something. So I began to try and understand what it was talking about. It is preceded by instructions to get yourself a brick, build a siege wall, raise up a ramp, and then get yourself an iron plate and set it up—as an iron wall. I had little difficulty recognizing this as a form of a bomb shelter and more evidence supporting of a nuclear holocaust.

We're told to strategically locate this between you and the city. Why is that? Chapter 5 of Ezekiel says: *"One third of you will burn in the fire at the center of the city."* I thought to myself, "Nuclear bombs will target cities, not vast expanses of mountains or agricultural land or anywhere else." Ezekiel informs us the people in the city will perish of famine and plague; another third will perish by the sword in the country. Apparently, the people in the country deal with a different problem than those in the city. Evidently, the plague that these scriptures foretell of has not spread out into the country at least not to a lethal degree, potentially because it is radiation sickness and that is not contagious. It will remain a problem for some time to come in the city.

The intensity of the famine is not as bad out in the country where the population is sparser, plus country people have farms and livestock.

I continued to think about that verse in Ezekiel Chapter 7 that says "the survivors will escape and they'll be on the mountains, with shame on their faces and baldness on their heads." Not only does radiation cause hair loss, but another thing about being in the mountains — there is a generous supply of uncontaminated fresh water coming out of the mountain springs that plays an important role for the survivors. We are told at the end of Ezeliel Chapter 4 that both food and water will be scarce.

SIMILAR SCROLLS

Further instructions are to set up a camp behind the iron re-enforced brick wall and get 390 days worth of stored food because food and water will be scarce. I was already familiar with scriptures in Revelations that say a "day's wages for a quart of wheat."

I began to see numerous similarities in Revelations and Ezekiel. At the end of Chapter 2 of Ezekiel, a hand reached out to him. In it was a scroll that had writing on both sides, and it's filled with words of lament, and mourning and woe.

Revelations 5 talks about a right hand that has a scroll in it, with writing on both sides of it. That scroll is filled with words of tribulation. The Lord made copies of the same end time scroll and passed them out not only to Ezekiel 2 and Revelation 5, but also Isaiah 8, Jeremiah 36, and Zechariah 5.

EZEKIEL'S INSTRUCTIONS

EZEKIEL 7:5   "AN END IS COMING"
A UNIQUE DISASTER IS COMING !
(THE DAY OF THE LORD)

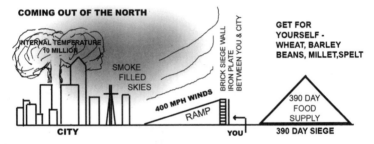

EZEKIEL 1:4
FIRE CLOUD INFOLDING
ITSELF

COMING OUT OF THE NORTH

INTERNAL TEMPERATURE 10 MILLION

SMOKE FILLED SKIES

400 MPH WINDS

RAMP

BRICK SIEGE WALL
IRON PLATE
BETWEEN YOU & CITY

GET FOR YOURSELF -
WHEAT, BARLEY
BEANS, MILLET, SPELT

CITY

YOU

390 DAY FOOD SUPPLY

390 DAY SIEGE

EZEKIEL 5:2

·FIRE INSIDE THE CITY-

<THIS IS A SIGN!!!>

FAILURE TO PAY ATTENTION MAY COST YOU YOUR LIFE.

THE FOUR JUDGMENTS

Ezekiel Chapter 14 tells us "The Lord has just four judgments—the sword, the famine, the plague and the wild beast." Those same four judgments are listed in Chapter 6 of Revelations, as the seals on that scroll opened. Out come the four horsemen called the riders of the apocalypse, and they are given power to kill by sword, famine, plague and wild beasts. By paying careful attention, the four judgments can also be found in Leviticus chapter 26 along with verse 24 that refers to the seven years of coming tribulation. Wherever these four judgments are found all together, it is a sure way of easily recognizing that those passages of scripture are referring to the unique disaster at the time of the end.

Leviticus 26:21-26 (New International Version)

21 "If you remain hostile toward me and refuse to listen to me, I will multiply your afflictions seven times over, as your sins deserve." (The seven times is the coming seven years of Tribulation/World War III.)

22 " I will send <u>wild animals</u> against you, and they will rob you of your children, destroy your cattle and make you so few in number that your roads will be deserted."

23 "If in spite of these things you do not accept my correction but continue to be hostile toward me."

24 "I myself will be hostile toward you and will afflict you for your sins seven times over."

25 "And I will bring <u>the sword</u> upon you to avenge the breaking of the covenant. When you withdraw into your cities, I will send <u>a plague</u> among you, and you will be given into enemy hands."

26 " When I <u>cut off your supply of bread</u>, ten women will be able to bake your bread in one oven, and they will dole out the bread by weight. You will eat, but you will not be satisfied."

And Deuteronomy Chapter 29:23 warns that the "whole land will be a burning wasteland" similar to the destruction of Sodom and Gomorrah. Chapter 32 goes on to say the fire has been kindled by the wrath of God and verse 20...and see what their end will be...makes clear reference, that the context pertains to this time of the end.

"*I will send a wasting famine against them, consuming pestilence and plague,*" it says.

Once again, we discover the radiation dust described as follows: "*...venom of vipers that glide in the dust.*" To put it mildly, radiation dust bites people, leaving them covered with sores.

In Verse 35 the Lord proclaims that their "*foot will slip, their day of disaster is near, their doom rushes upon them.*" Ultimately, the Lord shall judge his people, showing compassion to his servants.

Ezekiel 12:1 "*Say to them, I am a sign to you, as I have done, so it will be done to them!*" Co-incidentally what happened to me was exactly that, my foot slipped, and I experienced a day of disaster unlike anything that had ever happened to me before. I hope and pray such a thing never happens to me again. As my left arm and leg were suddenly shattered—so it will be just as devastating to this country on the Day of the Lord. I have had a long and slow recovery process, and I am now in pretty good shape. America will also have a long and slow recovery period, and then she will emerge as the champion of the world!

The Bible tells us in no uncertain terms within the New Testament that at this time of the end, people will be busy "buying and selling; and building and planting; and marrying and giving in marriage when sudden destruction comes upon them." This depicts a complacent society where people are caught up in a forward-moving fast paced economy. Instead we should be sober and vigilant—not caught up in the cares of this life.

Because the Lord has shown me these things, I've been alarmed every single year since 1999. Everything I've discovered has been confirmed by the hand of God, and points to this end-time disaster. It is because of His grace and mercy toward us, He is revealing his plans to those who have a heart to hear the truth. The truth will set you free and knowing what is coming is crucial to surviving. But you have to take action, for Isaiah 32:8 says the noble man makes noble plans and by noble deeds he will stand.

RADIATION CONTAMINATED FARMLAND

"The fields are ruined, the grounds dried up, the grains destroyed," says Joel Chapter 1 as it describes what it will be like on the "Day of the Lord". It warns us that the vine growers wail because their vines are dried up; the farmers despair for the wheat and barley because the harvest of the field is destroyed. The herds of cattle wonder about, moaning for their pasture is taken away

Jeremiah Chapter 8 gives a similar forecast about taking away their harvest, and the leaves on the trees will wither, (more evidence of the nuclear winter) and give them poisoned water to drink; adding that *"what I've given them will be taken away from them."* The Lord will allow all this to happen because we've sinned against him. The Bible tells us that this shall become evident to many people when they see that the summer ends and the harvest is passed, and yet they still aren't saved. Even Jeremiah laments that *"since my people are crushed, I am crushed,"* mourning and gripped in horror. He mourns partly because there's no balm or ointment to heal sores, such as those caused from radiation.

Besides storing foods, we should also stockpile medical supplies of every kind. One that might be particularly useful is healing salves such as Neosporin® ointment to stop infections and treat seeping radiation sores. For the most part, a vast majority of Americans remain ignorant about radiation fallout—how to detect it and its symptoms.

Another useful ointment to have is the stuff that treats athlete's foot. Many people may be walking and unable to change their socks or even take showers for days, resulting in that kind of burning and itching affliction. The scriptures tell us that for a lack of knowledge, people shall perish. Those traveling without Geiger counters risk entering into death zones of highly radioactive areas, exposing themselves to high radiation without knowing it. A noble plan would be to acquire a radiation detection device.

Revelations 6 tells us that a black horse emerges carrying a scale for carefully measuring every morsel, as men become willing to work an entire day for a quart of wheat as wages.

Starving families shall struggle to eat, resigning themselves to work for just enough food just to stay alive because at that time nothing else will matter. Numerous scriptures foretell of extreme hunger even to the degree of cannibalism in some places. But you need not allow yourself to be found in that kind of a gruesome scenario.

WHAT IS GOING TO HAPPEN

In Second Peter II we are told that the Lord condemned Sodom and Gomorrah by burning them to ashes AND He made them an example of "what is going to happen" to the ungodly. The fire fell from the sky and burned them up. That is an example of thermal nuclear fire, and that is what is going to happen. It is a clear example of today's modern cities that are going to burn.

2 Peter 3:6-7 notes that the world was deluged by water in Noah's day, while the present heavens and earth are reserved for judgment by fire and the destruction of ungodly men.

In fact, as these scriptures describe it, the "ungodly" people are primarily the ones within our society who will face the brunt of the attack. Isaiah 3:10 tells us that righteous people will do well, enjoying the fruit of their deeds—deeds of preparations of stocking up.

Isaiah 32:8 says "But the noble man makes noble plans, and by noble deeds he stands."

I want you to be a noble man and make your plans to deal with these difficult times so you can stand and persevere through them.

Isaiah 32:10 says "In a little more than a year [the same 390 days of siege in Ez. 4:4] people who once felt secure will tremble, their grape harvests will fail and their fruits will not ripen." This is what happens in June, the apples are small and green but the leaves wither from the nuclear winter the crop of apples is lost and the tree goes dormant until the next spring. A new crop is on the way.

Here again other scriptures support the reason Ezekiel 4 instructs you to prepare by storing up 390 days supply of food.

Mulituple scriptures appear to support the domino effect of a nuclear holocaust resulting in a harvest that is contaminated by fallout dust.

Isaiah 33 "People will get burned as if to lime." Lime resembles white dust. What do you suppose could turn a human body into a pile of white dust? The million-degree heat of a nuclear blast will instantly incinerate people. Isaiah 33 continues by saying that sinners are terrified, trembling grips the godless. Who can dwell with the consuming fire? The answer is a righteous man who dwells in a mountain fortress. His food and water will be supplied. Remember that Ezekiel 7 said all who survive and escape will flee to the mountains. Nevada is considered the most mountainous state of the lower forty-eight.

The fallout dust that covers the environment will be rinsed off the upper elevations first and become concentrated in the water shed in the lower elevations making the water in lakes, creeks, rivers, and reservoirs poison to drink. Those living at higher elevations are better off than those at sea level. The surface waters may be contaminated, but underground water in domestic wells should remain potable. Because we have been told that the nation's power grid is vulnerable to attack, consider this as a primary reason to have generators to power up pumps in wells.

THE UNIQUE DISASTER

I cannot emphasis the importance of these scriptures enough. In the New International Version, Ezekiel 5:9 proclaims that the Lord will bring his wrath. "Because of all your detestable idols, I will do to you what I've never done before and never will do again." This disaster is the end-time unique disaster of Ezekiel 7:5 NASV.

This end-time disaster consists of these four punishments: famine, the sword, the plague and the wild beast. And as we've said, Chapter 5 reiterates that a third of the people will perish by famine and plague inside the city,

Another third will fall by the sword, killed outside, in the country—"*a third I will scatter to the winds and pursue with a drawn sword."* The third that survives is scattered and pursued by their attackers with swords. All who survive and escape will be in the mountains, moaning like doves of the valley, and their heads will be bald, (because radiation causes hair loss), and the wild beasts will bereave them of their children.

THE SAME TWO THIRDS

Zechariah 13:8 warns that two thirds will be struck down and perish; yet one-third will be left and survive. The Lord will bring them into the fire. *"They'll be refined, purified, and call on the name of the Lord."* These are the same two thirds and one third in Ezekiel 5:12. Many similarities, coupled with those I've already told you about, describe "the time of the end," all confirming the same conclusion.

Those who will survive are the righteous—those who seek to purify themselves for the Lord. "One third will be left, and this third I will bring into the fire, and I will refine them like silver—test them like gold. They will call on my name, and I will answer them. I will say they're my people, and they'll say, 'The Lord is our God.'"

This is a refining fire, a purifying process, but these people will emerge from the fire without being incinerated or burned, and they're going to survive. Furthermore, Isaiah 26:9 declares, "When the judgments of the Lord come upon the earth, people of the world will learn righteousness." Without question, the Lord is going to teach us one way or another. Ultimately, as heartless as this might sound, you're either going to learn, or you're going to burn. The Lord and his messengers in the Bible make this clear. Thus, it's up to us to follow his path and benefit from these teachings.

So, take heed when considering Jeremiah Chapter 7, says to reform your ways and your actions, and I will let you live in this place.

Second Peter II states that we should live holy, godly lives as we await the day of the Lord: *"In speed, it's coming. That day will bring about the destruction of the heavens by fire."* And as is the case with a thermal nuclear bomb, "the elements will melt in the fervent heat." In keeping with his promise, you can look forward to a new heaven, a new earth, the home of the righteous. Just as Ezekiel 18 says *"It is the soul who sins that will die." These scriptures refer to the coming new age—the 1000 years of peace on earth.*

THE COMING
390 DAYS OF SIEGE

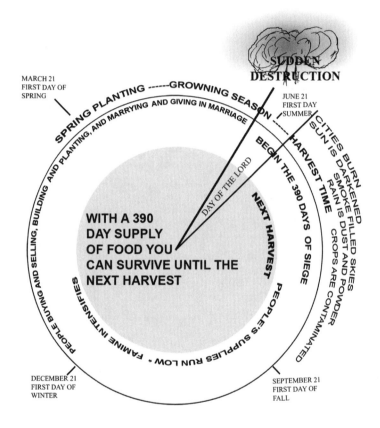

OBEY THE INSTRUCTIONS IN GOD'S WORD
GET YOUR SUPPLIES NOW WHILE YOU CAN

CHAPTER 5

THE FOUR HORSEMEN OF THE APOCOLYPSE

The Bible's Book of Revelation Chapter 6 describes the Four Horsemen of the Apocalypse. Each plays an integral role to the overall message you've learned about here:

When the first seal broke, *"...out came thunder, and I looked, and I saw there before me was a white horse, and its rider held a bow, and he was given a crown, and he rode out as a conqueror bent on conquest."*

Thunder is the sound of the detonating bombs on the "Day of the Lord." The rider on the white horse represents our enemies coming to conquer us. There is forming an alliance of enemy nations who intend to challenge the United States for world domination. While claiming that we violated international law when we attacked Iraq based on faulty intelligence, they're saying our days are over. We must be brought to justice. It may very well be an attempt to enforce international law and authorized by the United Nations. I suspect that ever since the remark was made about "shock and awe" they have been planning to teach us just what real "SHOCK AND AWE" are.

1 WHITE HORSE: The voice of thunder is the sound of exploding nuclear bombs, the Day of the Lord—the beginning of World War III. This horse's color is bright white, like the brilliant light emitted by an exploding nuclear mushroom cloud, and the rider rides forth bent on conquest. The enemies of America are rising up to challenge us for the future of the whole human race. This horse is immediately followed by the:

2 RED HORSE: The rider comes forth with a sword representing the outbreak of war. The red depicts the blood

shed when many slain bodies are lying on the ground on the Day of the Lord. This horse is followed by the:

3 BLACK HORSE: The rider carries scales that represent famine and a day's wages for a quart of wheat. The black color represents mold and mildew on spoiled food.

4 ASH/PALE HORSE: Brings the plague, which we know from linking other scriptures to it comes as radiation sickness caused by fallout ash—the color of the horse.

These four horses bring the same four judgments described in Ezekiel—the sword, famine, plague and wild beasts. They come in sequence one after the other. This is a major piece of information now given to us. We are told that these four horses are given power to kill by the same four judgments listed in Ezekiel 14:21, being the sword, famine, plague, and wild beasts. But their power to kill is limited to only a certain portion of the earth. You will be informed about the explanation of that later.

Ecclesiastes 7:27 from the Bible says that *"Adding one thing to another to discover the scheme of things"*. It is as simple as putting pieces of an amazing end-time puzzle together by adding one verse to another. Once a puzzle nears completion, the remaining last pieces are easy to fill in.

BEWARE OF MOUNTAIN LIONS AND BEARS

After reading in Ezekiel Chapter 7 that all who survive and escape will flee to the mountains, and there the wild beasts will bereave them of their children, I thought it doesn't seem like it could be describing our modern civilized country. With lingering doubts in my mind about who these scriptures are foretelling of, I put my Bible away and turned on the television.

A program on the television was about a game warden in an elementary school classroom telling the children that the mountain lion population has exploded and that they are potential prey for mountain lions since they're smaller than adults. "A mountain lion is less likely to take down a six-foot-tall man than a child," the game warden said. The children were instructed to not run if they encounter a mountain lion, but to stand and face it with both arms raised to appear larger. To run would trigger the predator instinct causing the mountain lion to pursue.

Those who flee to the mountains will be entering the domain of the mountain lion. As far as the mountain lions are concerned dinner is now served. After seeing this program, I knew the Lord confirmed to me that He has everything ready and in place for His word to be fulfilled. Since that program I have seen numerous front page newspaper stories about record number of bear encounters including a boy who was dragged away in the middle of the dark night and his remains were found the following day. This is just the beginning of a very real problem we will face in this coming time of the end. One way to be prepared is to pack a large caliber pistol with plenty of ammo.

The scriptures also designate specific types of events in various geographic locations. A third of the people will perish in the cities by famine and plague, *"but the plague is not contagious because they aren't perishing in the countryside from it."* The famine is more severe in the city because the population is concentrated and the supplies are cut off.

SWORD IN THE COUNTRYSIDE

By paying careful attention to Ezekiel Chapter 5, we can see that the four judgments are not all in the same place. In the country, there are fewer people and more food. Apparently the people in the country aren't dying from famine or plague. In the country there are farms with livestock and grain silos, more food and less people. The plague being radiation sickness and not contagious is not a problem in the country because the city is too far away for the radiation to be a deadly problem, but they will be at risk of perishing by the sword.

In addition to attacking and invading armies, desperate starving city dwellers will begin to pillage the countryside. People living in the country go to the cities for supplies. But after the attack, the city has been reduced to rubble and not only has the source of supplies for the people in the country been terminated, but the now the people in the city will be coming out into the country looking for supplies.

In fact, Isaiah 33 specifically says that highways will be desolate—no travelers on the road. The United States has the greatest interstate highway system in the world. Our lavish lifestyle is sustained by the big trucks that keep all kinds of supplies distributed. In fact one day a truck in front of me had a bumper sticker on it that said "If This Truck Stops America Stops." Even the truckers know they are responsible for keeping us going. This explains Isaiah 3:1 the Lord will cut off all support and all supplies of food and water.

Isaiah Chapter 2 sets the timing of the context in the last days, and mentions the day of the Lord. Their land is full of silver and gold, *"no end to their treasures,"* and they bow down to the idols cleverly made by their hands. Our society is consumed with materialism. These scriptures are clearly applicable in describing today's society.

Therefore men shall flee *"to the caves and the rocks,"* and holes in the ground—which is excellent strategy for seeking shelter from radiation. Like a man suffering blistering heat in a barren desert seeks shade from a tree, those seeking relief from radiation exposure will hunt for underground shelter.

DISASTER FROM THE NORTH

I remembered Ezekiel 1:4 "I looked and behold a whirlwind coming out of the north. (Nuclear blast emits 400-mile-per-hour winds, nearly three times more powerful than 150-mile-per-hour Category 5 hurricanes) and an immense cloud of fire enfolding itself, surrounded by brilliant light."

When I decided to read the Book of Jeremiah, I began to recognize a connection between Ezekiel and Jeremiah, where in Chapter 1 the Lord tells him disaster will be poured out from the north and that the Lord will summon the kingdoms of the north.

Because I remembered Ezekiel's description of a mushroom cloud, and he said he saw it coming from out of the north, I'm convinced that it's the disaster—the unique and unheard of disaster—described in Ezekiel 7 that has never been done before, and will never be done again according to Ezekiel 5:9.

So, as I read Jeremiah he continues talking about this great destruction from the north, and the scorching wind, and the alarm of war, the whole land is devastated. And then it says, *"An army's coming from the land of the north."* North becomes one of the repeated identifiable characteristics of this one-of-a-kind event in our immediate and imminent future.

Because from Jeremiah 1:14, we learn that the Lord said that from the north, disaster will be poured out on all who live in the land.; once again we learn of an attack from the north, in a manner never done before, and which *"will never be done again."* Without question Jeremiah talks of the same disaster from the north that Ezekiel describes. Yet we can take comfort in the promise that *"they will fight against you, but not overwhelm you—for I will rescue you, declares the Lord."*

Jeremiah says all this will happen because we have forsaken the Lord. In our American society today, this rings true as the courts allow schools and governments to throw out or destroy any mention of the Ten Commandments. Worsening matters, authorities also have forsaken the word of God by prohibiting school prayer. Such deliberate policies have lead to disasters such as the shootings of many high school students in Columbine, Colorado.

In *Jeremiah 2:34*, we learn of the *"lifeblood of innocent poor upon your clothes,"* a verse often quoted at abortion rallies where people fight for rights of unborn children. Jeremiah also states that *"disaster will follow disaster,"* as the whole land lay in ruins— where people committed adultery, and they thronged in houses of prostitution, well-fed lusty stallions neighing for another man's wife. Jeremiah asks, *"Should they not be punished for this?"* but adds *"...do not destroy them completely."*

The United States of America is guilty of every single indictment that you can possibly find in the most thorough search

of Holy Scriptures. I challenge anyone to find a single exception.
Like a defense attorney tries to find a technicality or a loophole
to get his client off, I tried, but there are no such verses.

CHAPTER 6

WRITE A BOOK

I knew I had to write this book after I read Isaiah 30:8 *Go now, write it before them on a tablet, and inscribe it in a book, so that it may be for the time to come as a witness forever.*

TIMING REVEALED

I began to understand from Jeremiah 6 some timing information. It says they're planning to attack at noon, but that shadows grew long, the daylight faded—so they're going to make it a night attack.

I already knew verses in the New Testament about the Lord coming like a thief in the night. And on that night, two men will be in a field, one will be taken, and one will be left.

THE TRUTH ABOUT THE RAPTURE

For anyone who has false hopes of being taken away, as in the rapture, they need to take heed to Luke 17:37

"Where, Lord?" They asked. He replied, "Where there is a dead body, there the vultures will gather".

The one that gets taken is a dead body that the vulture gathers around. Ezekiel 18 says it is the souls who sin that will die and 2 Peter 3 tells us that the new earth will be the home of the righteous. For Zechariah 2 says the Lord is coming to dwell among us and here we will be with him.

Then, Jeremiah tells us that the Lord is going to take away the harvest. The leaves on the trees will wither, and He will give them poisoned water to drink. I knew that could be caused by radioactive fallout dust. I began to understand why Ezekiel says to store up food, with famine coming, caused by a harvest being contaminated by radioactive fallout dust.

But it occurred to me that for a harvest to be taken, it has to be out there—vulnerable. I'm from an agricultural valley, and I work for farmers. I recognized these scriptures also are important timing information. Harvest time is in the fall, and I knew that Jesus said no man knows the day or hour. I now know the harvest will not come, causing a sudden unanticipated widespread food shortage. Now you can make sense out of Ezekiel's instructions to get 390 days supply of food.

SAME ARMY FROM THE NORTH

I found Ezekiel 38 talking about Gog and Magog, Persia, Cush, Gomer, and others who come from their place in the far north. This is also another passage of scripture pertaining to the Day of the Lord.

It says they will come against the people in a land of unwalled villages, living peacefully and unsuspecting—without walls and gates and bars—gathered from the nations, rich in livestock and goods, living at the center of the land. The United States fits these descriptions.

Ezekiel calls the attackers *"a great horde and a mighty army."* The Day of the Lord in Joel 2 is also about a large and mighty army that comes, such as never was of old and never will be in ages to come. Before them, fire devours and behind them flames blaze. Before them, the land is like the Garden of Eden. Today's California has immaculately manicured vineyards and fruit orchards as far as the eye can see in every direction and is called the fruit basket of the world. It lies like the Garden of Eden.

They will attack us, but they will not be able to destroy us completely. We will recover; we will retaliate. We will prevail and emerge as the champions of the world.

Ezekiel 38 gives the same scenario. The invaders get turned around and fall in the mountains of Israel, which I know signifies mountainous regions of the United States. These areas range from the Appalachians and the Sierra Nevada to the Cascades, the Rockies, and other high-elevation areas. The large and mighty army of Joel's is later referred to the northern army that gets driven back out across a parched and barren land, and that is the land that they burned as they invaded.

Daniel Chapter 11:13 is also about this final conflict. The King of the North comes with a great horde against the King of the South.

This is all connected together. The Day of the Lord is referred to as a sudden destruction that comes upon unsuspecting people who are busy buying and selling; and building and planting; and marrying and giving in marriage.

All this happens while they're saying peace and safety, and sudden destruction will come upon them. Immediately following the Day of the Lord, the sun will be darkened, and the moon does not give its light. It's a day of darkness and gloom. It's the result of smoke-filled skies coming from the cities burning.

FALLOUT DUST IN THE BIBLE

Smoke is particles, soot, and ash rising high into the sky because of the heat of the fire. When the heat dissipates, these particles begin to float down. They're referred to as fallout.

One day I tried to share some of my newfound insight of end-time scripture with my wife, but she complained, "I'm sick and tired of hearing about doom and gloom. The Bible is a big book. Why don't you read something different once and awhile?"

I ignored her suggestion right then, and I continued reading. But that very night I awoke around two o'clock in the morning by the throbbing pain in my shattered leg. I couldn't sleep. So I decided to turn on the lamp and read my Bible. Right when I picked it up, the words my wife spoke to me earlier that day suggesting that I should read something different once in a while echoed in my mind. I thought, "Well, maybe she's right."

So, I turned near the front of the Bible far from anything I had been reading, and when it opened, the verse my eyes focused on was Deuteronomy 28:24. There I began to read, "*The Lord will turn the rain of your land into dust and powder. It will come down from the skies, until you are ruined."* I thought, "Can this be talking about fallout dust?"

So I backed up to read the preceding context and there it says the Lord will smite them with a wasting disease, fever, inflammation, blight, mildew, sores, tumors, scabs, and boils, and itch from which you cannot be cured. There is no cure for radiation sickness and I became convinced was what it is describing. This is what the scriptures say people will suffer as consequences of their disobedience.

Deuteronomy 28 starts out describing a nation that harkens diligently to serve the Lord and obey his commandments. That nation will be placed high above all nations on the earth. We above all the nations of the earth fit that description best. I became deeply convinced that God himself is consistently revealing to me through the Bible what is going to happen. So when I try to read about something different for a change, I find even more scriptures confirming the coming end-time distress.

Indeed, Deuteronomy goes on to say that those who survive will be given abundant prosperity, and their blessings are described on and on until it comes to a *"however"*—if they *"turn from following my commandments, these curses will come upon them."*

DANIEL 9:11 PREDICTS GREAT DISASTER

On another day, I was reading in the Book of Daniel and believe it or not, Daniel 9:11 says, *"Therefore, the curses and sworn judgments written in the Law of Moses*—which by the way includes of the Book of Deuteronomy—*have been poured out on us because we have sinned against you."*

"You have fulfilled the words spoken against us and against our rulers by bringing on us a great disaster. Under the whole heaven has never been done, like what has been done to Jerusalem."

So the coming great disaster of Daniel 9:11 is the curses of radiation sickness and fallout dust according to Deuteronomy 28!

I want to make a point about the name Jerusalem. It may have been the capital city in the time of Daniel. In visions of the future, Daniel may have seen a major modern capitol city and assumed it was what Jerusalem had evolved into. Time has a way of changing things. But in our capital city today of Washington, D.C. you see large fluted columns that are a trademark of Greek architecture. The first senators came from Greece and they were elected. We represent the Kingdom of Greece as it has evolved over time.

Daniel 11:2 tells of a forth king who will be far richer than all the others and by the power of his riches he will stir up everyone against the kingdom of Greece (USA).

New York City boasts itself as the capital of the World because of the United Nations headquarters located there.

But the point is like Shakespeare said, *"A rose called by any other name still smells the same."* We know this great disaster that's coming isn't coming upon today's Jerusalem because those people there don't dwell in a land of peace, whose cities have no walls — such as that referred to in Ezekiel 38:11.

Instead, the Jerusalem of today is a land of suicide bombers. One day I turned on the TV and Jerusalem was on the news and because of the violence, that city was building a forty-mile-long, twenty-foot-tall concrete tilt-up wall. These scriptures absolutely are not talking about today's Jerusalem.

"ISRAEL" REFERS TO THE UNITED STATES AND GREAT BRITAIN

We can see from various current and recent events, coupled with many Biblical references and descriptions, the term "Israel" or "Jerusalem" refers to the United States rather than the Holy Land. It is in fact more about a linage of people than about some particular piece of real estate with geographical boundaries. Past puzzling passages begin to make sense when you apply this logical insight.

By contrast, in a clear comparison to the United States we learn from Ezekiel 38 that the attacks from nations out of the north will hit a *"peaceful, unsuspecting people...all of them living without walls, and gates and bars."* This great horde will come to seize much plunder in a land that has recovered from war (The

Civil War) whose people are gathered from all nations, another obvious reference to the U.S.

I visited a large church in New York City that boasted of more that a hundred different nationalities represented in their congregation. As it says, we truly are gathered from all nations. The peaceful unsuspecting people that are attacked are rich in goods and livestock. Americans cannot deny that they are the richest nation in the history of the world. The good news is that the invaders from the north will fall on the mountains, and they will be given to the beasts of the field to be devoured. We are punished, but not completely destroyed. We will be rescued by the Lord according to Jeremiah 1:19.

I continued studying Deuteronomy, and I found the four judgments in Chapter 32—right before it says that the country targeted for attack is a *"nation without sense, and there's no discernment in them. If only they were wise and would understand this, and discern what their end will be."*

And it goes on to say, *"In due time, their foot will slip. Their day of disaster is near, and their doom rushes upon them."* In the same way that my foot slipped, and sudden disaster was upon me, and the Lord has shown me that now the proverbial foot of our nation will slip and the sudden disaster coming is the Day of the Lord. What do you think about that!

CHAPTER 7

WARS AND RUMORS OF WARS

Matt. 24:6 Jesus said, "You will hear of wars and rumors of wars, but see to it you are not alarmed. Such things must happen but the end is still to come."

On the same day I arrived home from the hospital to recover from my broken arm and leg, I picked up the remote and turned on the television. Breaking news: "The bombing of Yugoslavia was just beginning." Confined to my house by my injuries, I faithfully followed the news day after day, morning, noon, and night. So everything I began to understand literally cost me an arm and a leg.

I watched President Clinton explain in a nationwide address why we were bombing Yugoslavia. He said, "I have a moral obligation. I cannot morally stand by and do nothing, while Milosevic is perpetuating these atrocities in his country. My morals compel me to do something."

I immediately perceived that we were in big trouble if President Clinton's morals were the reason for the bombing of Yugoslavia. Right up to that time, the media had been going on and on about the Monica Lewinski scandal in the White House revealing the President's immoral character.

It appeared to me that out of desperation amid his crumbling moral image, President Clinton frantically looked around the world for a problem he could use to divert the national media's attention away from his embarrassing sexual affair.

BOMBING REKINDLES THE COLD WAR!

I watched numerous talk shows. Some tried to defend criticism of the United States by saying, "This is NATO bombing Yugoslavia." But others responded, "Make no mistake about it; it is the United States who is calling the shots."

I listened to an official Russian spokesman make a stern warning to the Clinton Administration: "You had better not do this. You're liable to rekindle the cold war, if not a hot one."

Yugoslavia is like Russia's little brother. The Russians certainly did not appreciate what was being done. But President Clinton was adamant that the bombing will not stop until the five-fold unilateral demands were met.

One day, on the news I saw some of the President's military advisors being interviewed; they expressed great frustration with President Clinton. They said he refused to take any of their advice. He insisted on the plan of continuously bombing only, at the rate of 600 sorties twenty-four hours per day, and nothing else. He was not willing to risk casualties from ground troops but using pilots at high elevation posed little risk. That was based more on a political than a military decision.

They said that never before in all the history of military warfare has anything like this ever been done before. I said to myself, "We're watching history in the making." These experts said they tried to tell him, "That's not how it's done." But they were talking to a man who had no military background or training. Yet the American people put him in charge, Commander in Chief of the most powerful military force the world has ever seen.

It's like telling a man who has never even been in a rowboat, "Here grab on and take over the helm of this mighty battleship. Take this baby out for a cruise and see how you like it." It was a recipe for disaster.

Then I slowly began to recognize that the bombing of Yugoslavia was foretold in ancient Bible prophecies. About that time, I began to read a story about a vision of a ram and a goat in chapter 8 of the Book of Daniel. Daniel says he saw a goat coming from the west, crossing the whole earth without touching the ground. The goat slammed into the ram in furious rage, trampling the ram.

No one could rescue the ram from the power of the goat. I thought, "This is the first time in all of military history that bombing exclusively is the only military action taking place. Well, we're not touching the ground, and we come from the west. We are called the men of the west. We fit the description of the goat."

I was witnessing the beginning of the fulfillment, of an end-time Bible prophecy. But who does it say the ram is? It just says that the ram had two horns. One of the horns was longer than the other, but it grew up later.

Daniel says: *"I watched the ram as he charged toward the west, the north, and the south. None could stand against him. He did as he pleased, and became great."*

The goat attacks furiously, striking the ram and shattering his two horns. The ram was powerless, and the goat knocks the ram to the ground and tramples him.

WHY WE FIGHT

While the bombing of Yugoslavia continued, one afternoon, I looked through a collection of videotapes we had that we never watched.

I picked one up that still had the cellophane wrapper on it. Little did I know that it would reveal who the ram is. The title was, "Why We Fight." I decided to watch the film that had been paid for by the Department of Defense. It was about the early stages of World War II, talking about the conflict being between the free world and the slave world.

That age old conflict has now resurfaced. In the interpretation of the vision of the ram and the goat we are told that the goat represents the kingdom of Greece and the ram represents the Medes and Persians. It is the Free Peoples of earth versus the kingdoms of slaves.

President Franklin Roosevelt had the movie, made to be played to the American armed forces, because at that time the prevailing mentality among Americans about the war was, "So what if the Europeans want to have a war. What do we care? Let them kill each other." It was called isolationism.

It showed actual footage of German troops invading Russia. It showed how Russia ultimately prevailed over the Germans and began pushing them westward all the way into East Germany, and pushed northward into Finland and southward through Hungry and Yugoslavia. This is the description of the ram.

The Russians did as they pleased and became great. Russia is the ram. The first horn is the Mother Country Russia, and the larger horn that grew later is the Russian satellite countries including Yugoslavia.

As the videotape concluded, it showed documented footage of Nazi warplanes flying over and bombing Yugoslavia. President Roosevelt came on the screen with a clinched fist, and he pounded his desk. He said about the Nazis:

"They have got to be stopped. We must stop them. They're dropping bombs from the air, and they're murdering innocent women and children."

As always, when a videotape ends, the television returned to its ongoing programming. I stared at the screen in disbelief, because now on the news I was still watching warplanes bombing the same country again, Yugoslavia. I thought poor Yugoslavia; they seem to always get the worst of it. Here they are getting bombed again.

But what are the odds of watching a video showing Nazi war planes bombing Yugoslavia—and then as soon as it's finished, the television that's connected to cable TV with forty-seven different channels available returns to it's ongoing programming, and there are American war planes bombing the same country, Yugoslavia? It was like history repeating itself.

During the 1999 bombing, officials were talking about innocent women and children being killed. Analysts and various retired military leaders dismissed this as unavoidable collateral damage, but instinctively

I knew in my heart Russian generals with clinched fists were pounding their conference tables in high level meetings, repeating FDR's words about the Nazi's bombing of Yugoslavia:

"They have got to be stopped. We must stop them. They're dropping bombs from the air, and they're murdering innocent women and children."

I was overwhelmed with these obvious signs that only God could be showing me.

OUR ENEMIES PROCLAIM WE'RE AN EVIL EMPIRE

Just as Roosevelt said that the Nazis must be stopped, today people in many countries worldwide consider the United States an evil empire that should be halted.

From their view, we're as self-serving, self-centered, and selfish as the Third Reich. For instance, our current detractors accused us of killing innocent women and children in Yugoslavia and in Iraq during the current war. We dismiss the deaths as unavoidable collateral damage.

Worsening matters, the leaders in various nations that oppose us are gaining their peoples' support, a growing unified opposition to our nation's very way of life.

Add to this people who embrace non-Christian religions who hate our beliefs, and you get a powder keg ready to blow sky high. Literally, it's as if a giant fuse has already been lit, to the nuclear bomb attack that is the "Day of the Lord."

And the goat became great, and at the height of his power the goat's horn is broken off. That is the sudden nuclear attack known as the Day of the Lord. Then, in its place four prominent horns grew.

Zechariah 1:18 also has four horns that scattered Israel, Judea and Jerusalem.

"Then, the Lord showed me four craftsmen, and I asked, 'What are these coming to do?' And he answered, 'These are the horns that scattered Judea so that no one could raise his head.'" But the Lord goes on to reveal that the craftsmen have come to terrify the horns of the nations and throw them down. The Lord knows I aspire to be one of those craftsmen.

INTERNATIONAL RESPECT FOR U.S. PLUMMETED

Worldwide respect for the United States deteriorated during the Clinton administration, largely due to his personal behavior, military tactics, and policies.

I became alarmed and convinced that I was witnessing end-time prophecies being fulfilled. For years bible scholars have tried to explain the vision of the ram and the goat. But it pertains to this time of the end, how could anyone get it right until it actually happens?

Countries worldwide continue polarizing against the United States. Those opposing our county, its people and policies include Iran, the Russian Federation, China, North Korea, France, and Germany—plus the United Nations Security Council, comprised of some of these same countries.

Not only during the NATO bombing of Yugoslavia in 1999, did Russia's hostility became apparent when a Russian official issued a stern warning to the Clinton Administration: "You had better not do this; you're likely to rekindle the cold war, if not a hot one!", but following NATO's bombing of the Chinese Embassy in Belgrade, where high-ranking Chinese officials were murdered, enraged demonstrators in Tiananmen Square proclaimed America as the new Hitler. Although the U.S. State Department offered apologies, and they claimed it was by mistake, the Chinese were seething with rage. And they still have not forgotten today.

During the Clinton Administration, a U.S. surveillance plane on patrol in the South China Sea collided with a Chinese fighter jet. The American plane made a forced emergency landing in that nation, where authorities held the American crew members as hostages. China completely dismantled the U.S. aircraft in an attempt to learn our technology and tactics, and that nation continues to harbor a deep-rooted growing animosity toward us.

The Chinese later shipped our plane back to us, dismantled in pieces in separate boxes. Such defiance marked just one of many instances of accumulating evidence that supports the claim that our enemies together are planning our eventual demise. Chinese leaders have openly announced that they will go to any length to keep Taiwan from becoming independent, even if it means nuclear war with the United States. All over the world, tensions continue to escalate.

North Korea continues developing a nuclear missile program, threatening America. Meanwhile, Russia President Putin supports Iran's nuclear program, despite U.S. President Bush's strong suggestions that the Russian Federation do otherwise. Terrorists have us in their cross hairs.

With encouragement and support from slave nations represented in its Security Council, the Secretary General of the United Nations condemned the U.S. attack on Iraq. Our action on Iraq has been declared illegal, although we deposed Saddam Hussein who killed tens of thousands of his own people. There were no weapons of mass destruction found. That being the justification for launching the attack, it appears to many that we jumped the gun—went off half-cocked so to speak. Enemies are now demanding that we must be brought to justice for breaking international law.

The United Nations has no international law enforcement capabilities, so when Saddam invaded Kuwait they looked to the United States to carry out that enforcement. But the authorization was limited to ending the aggression and removing Saddam from Kuwait.

US General Norman Schwarzkopf had approached First President Bush seeking authorization to use American forces to conduct an international law enforcement action. President Bush expressed concern about getting entangled in a long, drawn-out ordeal. He asked the general, "How long is this going to take?" Schwarzkopf's best estimate was approximately three weeks.

In developing their battle plans, U.S. General Schwarzkopf and then-General Colin Powell assessed enemy size and strength to be about 500,000. The generals established what has become known as the Colin Powell Doctrine, which states that you come at your enemies with overwhelming force.

With a coalition force of 750,000, Kuwait was liberated in just three days. Sudden action by U.S. armed forces decimated and pushed Saddam Hussein's troops back into their homeland. Due to the success of this operation, The Colin Powell Doctrine has become standard military policy today.

UNITED STATES ESTABLISHED A DANGEROUS PRESCEDENCE

Those plotting against the United States today will use the same strategy against us. Like we did to Iraq in the early 1990s, these adversaries want to invade the United States as quickly and as efficiently as possible with overwhelming, relentless force.

The U.S. established a dangerous precedence in early 2003. Based on erroneous reports that Iraq had weapons of mass destruction, we determined that to be sufficient justification to initiate an attack.

In the same way that we felt threatened by Saddam, how many of our enemies feel that we are a threat to them?

USE OF OVERWHELMING FORCE

Knowing that they feel threatened by us, they can now say they have sufficient justification to initiate an attack on us. As you'll soon discover in further detail, the scriptures state that we'll be attacked violently, suddenly, and without warning. It is called "The Day of the Lord."

Our enemies are developing a strategy to attack and destroy us. I know that plans are being laid, a strategy or tactic—the best way to destroy America, the sole remaining superpower. Trying to stop America is a big job. In the sequence of the story about the ram and the goat, the goat became very great. But at the height of his power, his large horn is broken off. That is the Day of the Lord, the breaking of America's military power by a devastating nuclear attack on multiple cities.

About the time the news revealed the bombing would continue at the rate of 600 sorties a day—a massive amount of destruction. My mind began to calculate—that's about one mission every two and one-half minutes twenty-four hours a day. This is an unusual display of military might that no other country could sustain or accomplish, and we continued the bombing for seventy-eight days.

During the bombing, I opened my Bible to read, and the verse my eyes focused on is the beginning of Chapter 33 of Isaiah. It says there, *"Woe to you, oh destroyer—you who have never been destroyed."*

I thought, "Who else is capable of dispensing a volume of destruction at the rate of 600 jet loads a day, and sustaining it for seventy-eight day's non-stop? That is more than 40,000 sorties. Who fits this description better than the United States, and world wars have come and gone yet we've not been destroyed."

But then it says, *"Woe to you, oh traitor, you who have never been betrayed."*

I could see how we could fulfill the description of the destroyer. But I didn't recognize us as being a traitor, until about that time I came across an article in the newspaper that said, *"Consider the irony of this, the Serbian people fought bravely on the allied side in both World War I and World War II."*

If this is how we treat our friends—nations who have fought bravely along side of us—what do you think our enemies are thinking we might do to them?

When the destroyer stops destroying, it says he'll be destroyed. Isaiah Chapter 33 also pertains to the end-time Day of the Lord because it continues on to say, *"The people are burned to lime."* Lime is just white dust. It says, *"The highways are desolate; there are no travelers on the road; who can dwell with this everlasting burning. Trembling grips the godless; the sinners are terrified."*

These are all descriptions that could be the result of a nuclear event. A verse in Ecclesiastes says understanding of a matter comes by adding one thing to another.

As I study, I continue looking for scriptures that add together and support this end-time disaster as a nuclear event.

A verse in Isaiah 33 catches my attention. It says, "Your breath will consume you like a fire."

I thought, "What it would be like to breath in radiation dust without a respirator or even a dust mask like those on construction jobs. Radiation dust if inhaled, will cause internal burning."

GO TO THE MOUNTAINS

Isaiah 33 says the righteous man will dwell on the heights; his refuge will be the mountain fortress. His bread and water will be supplied. And that's the same thing Ezekiel 7 says, "All who survive and escape will be in the mountains."

And Jesus talks about The Day of the Lord in Matthew 24: *"When you see the abomination that causes desolation."* Now there's an appropriate description of a nuclear bomb.

He gives instructions to those who are in Judea or Samaria, *"Let them flee to the mountains."* He says, *"Let no one on the roof of his house go down to take anything out of the house. Let no one out in the field go back to get his coat."*

To me, that means, "Immediately go." I see the major large cities being like the Atlantic City, N.J., nightclub where a musical group's pyrotechnics caught a crowded nightclub on fire. And all the people tried to get out at the same time. The exits became jammed. People were trapped and burned to death.

When a nuclear fire bursts forth in a city, all the people will panic and try to flee at the same time. Mass panic and hysteria will cause the on ramps to the freeways to have cars crashing into cars and become jammed. The people who attempt to gather their precious things lose the most important thing of all—precious time needed to get away, and they will be trapped and burn to death or suffer intense radiation exposure and die slowly. The verse says if you try to save your life you will lose it; if you lose your life you will save it. That verse seems difficult to understand, but it suddenly makes perfect sense when you think of your family photo albums, jewelry, etc. as your life in this kind of situation. You may lose all that stuff, but you might save your life if you flee immediately.

RUSSIA STILL IS

When the bombing of Yugoslavia stopped, I came across an article November 14, 1999 that said in discussing Chechnya, "It might seem presumptuous to tell a Russian leader what to do. But President Clinton did just that the other day in a dramatic confrontation with Russian leader Boris Yeltsin."

President Clinton said he didn't agree with how the rebellion in Chechnya was being handled. The article said, "Although President Clinton's words were offered in a spirit of tough love, President Yeltsin certainly didn't take it that way."

The Russians were horrified by the way we treated our past ally in two World Wars, Yugoslavia, when we didn't agree with how they were handling their internal ethnic problem. They could be wondering about what might happen to them, if we don't agree with how they are handling their internal problem of Chechnya.

Suddenly thereafter the international community is surprised by the announcement that Mr. Yeltsin is no longer to remain as the leader of Russia, but in his last days in office he visits China December 15, 1999 and says to the Chinese leader, "It seems Mr. Clinton has forgotten that Russia still is a world power that possesses a nuclear arsenal."

Now enters onto the scene Valadimir Putin, a trained KGB career man. His first two weeks in office on January 14, 2000 the Russian parliament changed their long-standing nuclear arms policy. The old policy only authorized the use of their nuclear weapons in the event of an attack on them. That is a defensive policy, using their nuclear weapons as a deterrent. The new policy allows the use of their nuclear power as a first strike in certain cases. That is an offensive policy and another sign that signals hostility brewing.

CHAPTER 8

GAY PRIDE PARADES

I continued to read Ezekiel 4 repeatedly in different translations. I'm convinced the instructions to build siege works between you and the city are a form of a bomb shelter, and the food storage all pertain—and are extremely relevant—to those of us upon whom this sudden end-time nuclear disaster will occur.

We're told to lie down on our left side, and put the sin of the house of Israel upon yourself. It says you are to bear their sins. At first I thought, "What kind of a raw deal is this. Why should you have to bear their sin?"

But then I was reminded that Jesus bore the sin of the whole world. Still, the question remained, "Who is the House of Israel?"

Isaiah 2 says, "Their land is full of silver and gold. There is no end to their treasures. Their land is full of horses; there is no end to their chariots. Their land is full of idols; they bow down to the work of their hands."

I thought of how materialistic our society has become. It says, "They're full of superstitions from the east, and they practice divination like the Philistines." At that time, there were numerous psychic advertisements on TV. Seems like today's society is a dead ringer for who it is.

Another thing happened that removed all doubt from my mind as I became convinced that the American people are whom these scriptures talk about. I had just finished reading and underlining Isaiah 3:9, where it says, *"they parade their sin like Sodom. Woe to them, they brought this disaster upon themselves."*

I recalled having heard and read about gay pride parades. And again I strongly suspected that we could be whom it's talking about. But, weary of reading the Bible, I put it away. And after resting a bit, I decided to pick up the remote and see what's on TV.

It had to be the Lord prompting me with impeccable timing, for when the television screen lit up, there on the channel it happened to be set on out of forty-even channels, was a hairy-chested man, wearing a stuffed red bra, prancing around with a streamer in his hand. It was on the news. It was the Reno Gay Pride Parade. I had just read the verse, where they parade their sin like Sodom. I had just pondered in my mind, "Could we be who this is talking about?"

I knew the Lord had immediately given me an affirmative answer. God has ways of showing you things, like in Genesis 24 and the story of Abraham's servant who was sent on a mission to find a wife for Isaac. He had just arrived at the community well after a long and hot day's travel. He prayed that if a maiden came to the well—and he asked her to draw water for himself; and she then would offer to also water the camels—that she would then be the one that he was supposed to take home to be Isaac's wife.

No sooner had he finished his prayer and opened his eyes than Rebecca came walking up to the well. He asked her to draw water for himself, and she then offered to also water his camels. He then told her how he had just prayed right before she walked up, and that she was the one the Lord had chosen to go away with him, leave her family and home, to marry a stranger she has never seen.

You might expect her response to be, "I don't know who you are, but if you think just because I offered to water your camels that I'm going to leave my home and family, to go some far away place with you, and to marry some stranger, you are crazy. But instead she immediately acknowledged that this is from the Lord. She then took him to her father's house, and when they told her family what had happened, they all agreed that this was the Lord. This story is an example of how God speaks, and it is the same way He has spoken to me over and over, as I am praying and thinking about something, then suddenly there is the obvious answer in an unusual and unexpected way.

When you see the confirmation of what you were immediately praying about suddenly materializes in front of your very eyes you can be sure that it is the Lord.

Like coming home from the hospital with a broken left leg and a broken left arm, praying about why this has happened to me, and then opening the Bible to Ezekiel 4:4, *"As for you lie down on your left side."*

Or it's like reading Ezekiel 1:4 about the immense cloud of fire, enfolding itself, surrounded by brilliant light—and thinking "Lord could this be describing a mushroom cloud?" And right then you hear at the door knocking an eighty-year-old man who comes in and explains how he was there and witnessed nuclear bomb tests. And he explains to you that the light is so bright they saw the bones in their arms as they covered their eyes to protect them from the blinding bright light.

Like reading Isaiah 3:9 about how they parade their sin like Sodom, and then while thinking this could be talking about today's society; I then put the Bible away to watch TV. And when you turn it on there is a hairy chested man wearing a stuffed red bra prancing around as the Reno Gay Pride Parade is proceeding down the main street.

Like watching the Nazi bombing of Yugoslavia only to see the video end, and then the news that is ongoing at that time has today's warplanes flying across the TV screen and bombing the same country.

I really can go on and on, but you will read about even more of these unusual and very convincing reasons why I know that God has shown me what is to come and even pertaining to the year this disaster will hit. It is upon us now.

I continued to read Ezekiel 4, repeatedly in different translations. I'm convinced the instructions about the siege works between you and the city, and the 390 days of food storage all pertain and are extremely relevant for those of us upon whom this sudden end-time disaster will hit.

It says for 390 days to lie there on your left side. It says get 390 days worth of food. Then, it says, *"I have assigned you the same number of days as the years of their sins."*

I began to suspect this could be a formula for telling the year that this will happen. After all, it doesn't make sense for God's word to give these kinds of instructions to prepare for a future coming disaster without any clue as to when this action should be taken.

But if the number of the days are the same number as the years of their sins, and we're being told the number of days are 390 — so the number of the years of their sins is also 390.

I began to have a question in my mind, "Did something happen 390 years ago that could be significant enough to be perceived as the beginning of the years of their sins? If we can determine what year the Lord begins to count the years of their sins, all we have to do is add 390 years to it, and we'll know the year that this disaster will take place."

HISTORY PROVIDES THE ANSWERS

I did not have a history book readily available, but I continued to lie around for several days with curiosity gnawing away at me about what could have taken place, if anything, of significance 390 years ago. I was thinking if I had a history book, I would check it out.

It so happened that about a year earlier, my oldest son had lost his American high school history book. And the end of the school year the school sent us a bill for it, which I had to pay before they would give him his report card. But nobody knew what had become of that book.

Now the Lord knew I was anxious to look back 390 years in our history and right at that time my daughter came downstairs carrying the same history book that he had lost. She had found it between the wall and the bed. I knew the Lord was providing me with it, and I asked her to bring it to me. I immediately opened it to check out what had been eating on me: "Did anything significant happen 390 years ago?"

The history book came alive with significant major events unfolding. King James was sending 600 men across the Atlantic with instructions to go start the first English colony. They were to name it Jamestown, in honor of the king, and the year was 1609. I thought, "Wow, this is very significant, it is the humble beginnings of our great nation. And now here we are- the greatest nation in the history of the whole world."

Then I decided to do a little math. (1999-1609=390).

390 years have passed since that initial major event. I literally freaked out. I figured time is up. As a businessman, I know numbers don't often fit easily unless they are supposed to. I became overwhelmed, recalling the Russian spokesman's warning to the Clinton Administration about the bombing of Yugoslavia, "You had better be careful or you're liable to re-kindle the cold war if not a hot one." Based on the timing of my newly discovered information, I became absolutely certain that the Russians were going to take us out. All I could do was to lie there in hopeless despair with a broken leg and arm. I couldn't go anywhere or do anything like buy supplies or get stocked up.

I was perplexed. Why would God show me these things in my injured condition, knowing I couldn't do anything about it? I wept as I contemplated our majestic America the Beautiful suffering simultaneous nuclear destruction in multiple major cities. As I wiped tears from my eyes, I closed the history book and the Bible. I set them aside. I can't stand to think about this anymore. It's too heavy burden to think about.

I reached for my remote control to turn on the TV, thinking I might find a Western movie or something to watch to take my mind off of these depressing thoughts. I pressed the power button on my remote; and I watched for the screen it to come on, but nothing was happening.

I glanced at the remote to see if its battery was dead or what. Why didn't it come on? Then after a short pause, I glanced back at the TV that appeared to be just a black screen that was not even on, suddenly a row of large white capital letters flashed on to the screen.

THE ATOMIC BOMB

These three words that appeared were the title to a program just beginning at that time and on that channel out of the 47 channels of cable TV available. I stared at those words, stunned by the coincidence. I was thinking what are the odds of this happening to me. It has to be that the Lord was showing me that this is what is coming even though I tried to escape from thinking about it, I now realized there is no escape. I instinctively knew this is what is coming right at us, NO ONE CAN STOP IT, and the blast of nuclear bombs is going to blow right over the top of us. We can prepare to deal with it, or we can choose to ignore it; but we can't stop it from coming.

STOCK UP ON WHEAT, BARLEY, BEANS, AND WATER

Ezekiel 4:9 warns us to stock up on enough food for 390 days or a little more than one year because food and water will be scarce. The basic food list is:

1 Wheat & Barley: Bread has remained the staff of life since Biblical times. It's essential for you to retain enough energy to survive. Besides using it for food, you could also store enough wheat to plant the following spring.

2 Beans and lentils: Other than meat, beans can help provide necessary proteins vital in sustaining life. As with wheat, you should store enough to eat for 390 days and enough to plant.

3 Water: Ensure that underground water wells remain operational. Not only will you need water to live, but it's also essential in growing crops. Well water is far less likely than surface water to be contaminated by nuclear fallout.

THE FORMULA FOR THE YEAR

Ezekiel says to put to sin of the house of Israel upon yourself, and that you are to bear the punishment for their sins for 390 days. It also says that you have been assigned the SAME NUMBER of days as the years of their sin. So, the 390 days of siege is the formula for the year. All we need to do to know what year this will happen is to figure out what year the Lord determines that the house of Israel began to sin and then add 390 years to it.

You will see that the most interesting of all is why, where, who, and what is happening within the time frame of 390 years ago. This 390-day formula moves ahead as you will see. I began to take notice that not only does it say, lie down on your left side for 390 days. It says after you finish this, lie down on your right side for forty more days and bear the sins of the house of Judah. Judah was the son of Israel.

Americans acknowledge England as their mother country, and because they came here to North America and started their first colony of Jamestown 390 years ago; they must be the house of Israel. That would make us sons of Israel. So, I also began to think about what was happening for the last forty years.

Ezekiel says the house of Judah will be punished for forty days: a day of punishment for each year of sin. And I thought, "It's easy. Forty years ago, the hippie movement began along with the spread of drug problems." That's when the "free love" era began due largely to the advent of the birth control pill, spreading immoral behavior that permeates American society even today. The 1960s became increasingly obvious to me as the start of this forty-year period of sin. There will be forty days of suffering coming to pay for the forty years of sin.

Ezekiel 8 describes what the house of Judah was doing. They were provoking the Lord to anger; there were twenty men of the House of Judah in the temple, between the entrance and alter with their backs turned to the Lord. They were bowing down to the east.

I can recall that Eastern religions became popular in our culture along with the hippies and the drugs during the 1960s. Ezekiel continues to say, *"Have you seen this, the detestable things they're doing here, filling the land with violence and continually provoking me to anger. Look at them, putting the twig to their nose."*

The country was experiencing shootings, like in the Columbine School. I heard news reports about statistics revealing ninety percent of the violent crimes in our country are drug-related. And they are "putting the twig to their nose" is likely a description of snorting cocaine or crack, a common form of drug abuse today.

There has been a deteriorating change in morality in our country over the last forty years. The highest court in the land declared that it is against the law to pray in school. This is totally contrary to the constitution that says Congress shall make no law restricting the freedom of religion or the practice thereof.

Praying is talking to God and certainly an act of practicing one's religion, but the Supreme Court declares that it is now against the law to pray in school. So not talking to God is the same as turning our backs on Him.

As a nation we entered into an era where the schools have been left without a prayer. Days of being in trouble for chewing gum in class are gone, and the days of shooting guns in class have come. Previously unheard of but now common are drive by shooting and snipers killing innocent victims at random. Each and every line of these verses without exception depicts today's society with alarming accuracy.

FORTY YEARS OF SIN CONFIRMED

In September of 1999, I attended a Promise Keepers revival conference for men in Stockton, California.

Promise Keepers hosts many gatherings nationwide in sports arenas and football stadiums, capable of hosting 20,000 to 30,000 people. There were four speakers that day, two in the morning and two in the afternoon. I was standing in the back where they were selling refreshments with my Bible open, pointing to the verses in Ezekiel. I was telling other Christian men about how my left leg and left arm had been broken, and I showed them the verse that I turned to as soon as I came home from the Hospital that says, *"Lie down on your left side under siege for 390 days."*

And I told them that I had discovered that this is talking about us—that 390 years ago our country is beginning with the first English colony, and that the forty-year reference pertains to our present-day society, the baby boomer generation. I was explaining to them that THIS IS A SIGN, and that Ezekiel says that it's a sign right before it says, *"Lay on your left side."*

"The Lord is revealing to me these scriptures, and they all fit us," I told them.

I explained to the men in Stockton how the Book of Ezekiel is telling us when the end will come by coinciding of the accumulation of the 390 years of sin, and the forty years of sin. Strangely enough those numbers have significant application to us today.

Then as I was just finishing trying to convince my listeners about my interpretations, the Lord gave me a confirming sign that I was definitely onto the true meaning of these scriptures.

The founder of the Promise Keepers movement, Bill McCartney, a former college football coach, was the last speaker. He began to talk about how American society has been drifting away from the Lord for the last forty years. McCartney spoke for thirty minutes about the decade of the 1960s, and then thirty minutes about the '70s, followed by similar attention to the '80s and the '90s. I felt a strange sense of confirmation as I listened to him. I knew that the Lord was showing me that I was not alone in recognizing that the forty years of sin in Ezekiel pertains to the last forty years in our time.

It is like a map index that gives reference to a particular location. The map has letters across the top and numbers down the side. You see we are being given two sets of years that point to when this sudden disaster will hit like the two references on a map. If the map index is G-7 for instance you line up below the letter G and over from the number seven and you have a close proximity to the place you wanted to look for. We are in the time that is called "NOW." We know that the "NOW" is steadily moving toward the time of the end. When the "NOW" is the time of the sudden disaster there will be an undeniable and obvious beginning sin taking place 390 years ago. And as a second reference point at that same time there will also be 40 years ago also the beginnings of obvious and identifiable sin.

How do we know what qualifies as "identifiable sin?" Ezekiel chapter 8 gives us explicit descriptions of the sins they are doing. Hang in there and keep reading because much more on that is coming.

CONFIRMED AS AN APPOINTED WATCHMAN

As that Saturday Promise Keepers meeting came to an end, I stood in the middle of the football field with my cane while people were leaving all around me. Because of the injuries I suffered that spring my broken leg had not healed completely, I fought back the pain while thinking how am I going to get to my truck that was parked a least a mile away. As I stood there resting from the pain of each step, two ladies wearing Promise Keeper badges approached me, and they asked me if I was waiting to be prayed for.

"No," I said, "I am resting my sore leg that has been broken, but hasn't healed." I told them they could pray for the pain to ease and for it to heal. As the one lady finished praying for the Lord's healing power to touch my leg, the other lady began to speak the following words to me. She said, "The Lord has called you to be a watchman; He has given you an important job to do. You are to take this job seriously and not cast it aside, but to be faithful to carry it out and not to neglect it".

I began to cry because I knew the verses about the watchmen are in Ezekiel 3, right before Chapter 4, where "Lie on your left side" is. I then shared with them the story of my left arm and left leg being broken simultaneously, and how I came home and opened the Bible to the verse that says lie down on your left side.

I do not know their names and have never seen them again, but they called a golf cart to come over, and I was given a ride right up to where my truck was parked a half a mile away. The Lord does take good care of me, and He has shown me who I am. He even sent total strangers to tell me, so that all doubt about it is now gone.

CHAPTER 9

NO MAN KNOWS THE HOUR OR THE DAY

Even though the Lord has confirmed to me through other sources that we absolutely are whom these scriptures are talking about, the Day of the Lord obviously didn't occur in 1999.

But at the end of that year, as I watched TV on New Year's Eve, two pastors were being interviewed about the threat of Y2K that was looming. Many people were concerned. The pastors were asked, "Could this Y2K event be what the Bible talks about?" One pastor responded by saying, "No way. We're told that no man knows the hour or the day. So it cannot be midnight on New Year's Eve."

The other pastor said, "But we do know the time is at hand because II Peter 3 talks about the present heaven and earth are reserved for fire, kept for the day of judgment and the destruction of ungodly men. But we're not supposed to forget one thing. With the Lord a day is like 1,000 years and 1,000 years are like a day."

He explained that from the beginning of Adam until the time of Noah, approximately 2,000 years passed. This is the first age. From the time of Noah till the time of Jesus, another 2,000 years had passed. This is the second age. And from the time that Jesus came till now a third set of 2,000 years had passed. This is the third age and we are approaching the end of it.

That's 6,000 years, and the Bible talks about the New Age—the millennium being 1,000 years of peace on earth. He explained that in God's economy of time there are six days of work, and then the seventh day is the day of rest.

I liked that explanation, because the work is the harvest. We are told the harvest is at the end of the age. And when it's time for harvest, we're going to first gather the tares or weeds and burn them. And then we'll put the wheat into to the barn — the tares being the ungodly, and the wheat being the righteous.

We're told that we should look forward to the Day of the Lord, and in speed it's coming—for elements will melt in the heat (more evidence of nuclear activity). Even though the elements will melt in the heat, we are looking forward to a new heaven, a new earth, and the home of the righteous.

That same New Year's Eve, various TV broadcasts also mentioned one of the major events occurring in the last 100 years. In recapping the previous century, they mentioned a significant milestone in the advancement of the human race. In 1960, the birth control pill became available and widely distributed, and it caused a sexual revolution.

I went back to the history book, and reread about how the original 600 Englishmen who came, and only sixty of them survived. By the spring of 1610, they had abandoned the colony and were going down the James River when they met more ships just arriving from England. And they were turned around in an attempt to establish this colony. So, I adjusted my reasoning that in 1609, the colony didn't begin. It was only a failed attempt to establish a colony. I decided that the colony really became established in 1610 because 1999 had come and gone, 390 years later the end-time disaster hadn't happened.

So I became convinced that the introduction of the birth control pill in 1960, plus forty years adds up to the year of 2000 —and the starting of the colony in 1610 plus 390 years adds up to the year 2000 as well. I continue to tell all my friends, business associates, and family members that the Lord has told me what's going to happen. America is going to suffer a multiple nuclear attack. Only a few agreed with me. I began to understand that the Lord had appointed me as a watchman who is sent to stubborn and obstinate people who are not going to listen to me because they're not listening to the Lord.

I will try to share with you the process of the many events as they accumulated in my mind that convince me that I need to be warning everyone about what's coming. I felt the burden of the watchman, who is told, "If you don't tell them, you will be held accountable. Their blood will be on your hands."

WORLD EVENTS SIGNAL END OF THIS AGE

In late 1999, Russian leader Boris Yeltsin, to the surprise of the international community, suddenly announced his retirement.

I thought, "Maybe he's just not up to the job that they're talking about, being that of destroying the United States with a nuclear attack" With just two weeks left in office, one of his parting statements to the leader of China on Dec. 15, 1999, was: *"It seems Mister Clinton has forgotten that Russia still is a world power who possesses a nuclear arsenal."* I am convinced the Russians did not get over the bombing of Yugoslavia and neither will the Chinese get over the bombing of their Chinese Embassy in Belgrade that took the lives of important diplomats, even though the State Department offered apologies and claimed it was a mistake.

Not quite a month later on January 14, 2000, after new Russian leader Vladimir Putin took over the position of leadership, the headlines read: "Russia Reverses Longstanding Nuclear Policy." That nation now has authorized the use of their nuclear weapons as a first strike, reversing a longstanding policy that had stated their nuclear arsenal was strictly for defensive purposes.

Because of these brewing signals in addition to what I already had been shown by the Lord, I was convinced they were preparing to initiate a nuclear attack on America in the middle of the year 2000. I frantically tried to warn everyone, but the attack didn't happen.

You see, when a new leader assumes power, he immediately pursues the priorities of his agenda. I recall President Clinton doing that. Upon taking office in 1992, one of the first things Clinton did was to try to get the military to reverse its policy concerning homosexuals, resulting in, what was called the don't ask don't tell, policy.

By contrast, one of the first things Putin's Parliament did was to reverse that country's nuclear arms policy. The long-standing policy stated that Russia's nuclear weapons were authorized for use only if they were attacked first, and then in retaliation they would nuke their attacker. This policy served as a deterrent from a defensive stand.

The new policy allows the option of use of their nuclear weapons as a pre-emptive strike if they feel sufficiently threatened. This new policy is the opposite of a defensive stand and does in fact authorizes them to take an offensive position.

I have watched the pieces moving into place; the stage is being set; events are taking place that no man can change. It is now time for the fulfillment of all these things.

THE BIBLE PREDICTS THE SEASON

I began to understand what is going to happen because Jeremiah 8 tells us: *"The Lord is going to take away their harvest, and give them poisoned water to drink. The leaves on the trees will wither."*

This is occurring as the result of nuclear fallout. Scientists call it a nuclear winter. And Ezekiel 5:9 says, *"Because of all your abominations, the Lord is going to do the likes of which has never been done before, and will never be done again."*

I began to see the positive side of that. It's talking about a crop failure caused by radiation contamination that happens like Isaiah 18 says, before the Harvest—390 days of siege, following the nuclear attack will bring you full circle in the annual cycle to the time of harvest again the next year, and the food supply will then be replenished.

By adding forty more days makes a total of 430 days. Certain varieties of crops require a longer growing season. Numerous other passages confirm this. In Isaiah 32, it says that in *"a little more than a year, you who feel secure will tremble; the grape harvest will fail, and the harvest of fruit will not come."* Verses like these open up your understanding to the fact that the entire context before and after are also pertaining to this same end-time of distress, like Isaiah 33...people are burned to lime (pile of white dust, thermal nuclear fire).

ADD YEAR TO YEAR

Like a hammer that taps on a nail to start it, then a driving blow slams it home, the Lord drives my understanding a little deeper with Isaiah 29:6

"Suddenly, in an instant, the Lord Almighty will come with thunder, and earthquake, and great noise, and whirlwind, and with tempest and the flames of a devouring fire, a complete list of the characteristics of an atomic bomb with internal temperatures reaching up to ten million degrees and winds of four hundred miles per hour."

After I recognized what this passage of scripture was describing, I scanned the preceding context starting with the beginning of the chapter. I was astonished with the discovery of Chapter 29 of Isaiah because it begins with "ADD YEAR TO YEAR." It was a confirmation to what I had already been doing- adding the 390 years together to see when this will happen. And then more of the same words I recognized from Ezekiel Chapter 4 like besiege—set up siege works—encamp convinced me further. Then suddenly, in an instant, (like a detonating bomb), the Lord will come with the atomic bomb. These instructions from Isaiah 29 to add year to year certainly pertain to Ezekiel's formula that the number of the days of siege are the same number as the years of their sin.

Again the Holy Spirit has led and guided me to one scripture after another like someone who is completing a "connect the dots" puzzle. The verses connect one to another and the outline of the end time events are very real and confirmed to me.

The Lord is now ready to fulfill all these things I know, because He has revealed his plans to me just as Amos 3:7 says:

"*Surely the sovereign Lord God will do nothing, without first revealing His plans to His servants, the prophets.*"

I understood—a little more than a year—to be talking about the 390 days of siege in Ezekiel 4. That had never been done before and will never be done again. In Joel 1, it says, "*...despair you farmers over the loss of the wheat and the barley because the harvest of the field is destroyed. The fig tree is withered; all the trees are dried up*" and the context soon tells that it is all about the "*Day of the Lord*"

Isaiah 18 says the "*birds will feed on them all summer.*" I focused on the words "all summer," and I thought if you work all day you've started at the beginning of the day. I began to understand that this disaster is going to happen somewhere around the beginning of the summer. But I became totally convinced, as I was reading Matthew 24 where the disciples asked Jesus, "*Tell us when this will happen*"—talking about the end of the age.

Jesus answered, "*Learn the parable about the fig tree and all the trees. When you see the leaves come out, and the branches are tender, by this you know that summer is near. When you see these things, behold it is right at the door.*"

So it is very simple- when summer is near it is at the door.

SIGNS FROM THE SUN AND THE MOON

So, even though he goes on to say, "No man knows the hour or the day," he is definitely telling us exactly which month this will happen. The sun is the indicator of when summer begins; it's the summer solstice, the longest day of the year.

Genesis 1:14: "*...the sun and the moon are not only for separating the night from the day but are also to serve as signs.*" Signs that indicate when the time of the end will come is what it means, because this anticipated sudden destruction comes at night during the phase of the new moon and at the time of the year when the sunshine of the days are the longest. That is when summer is near.

THE YEARS ADD UP TO GREAT CAUSE FOR CONCERN

So, this verse about "add year-to-year" verified to me that I was doing the right thing by adding the 390 years to 1610 and the forty years to 1960 and coming up with the year 2000. I thought, "That would be just like the Lord, to bring the whole world to a point of great concern—such as the Y2K event and then have nothing happen."

This would make people think that it's clear sailing from here on out. But 1Thessalonians 5:3 says, *"While people are saying, 'peace and safety,' destruction will come upon them suddenly as labor pains on a pregnant woman and they will not escape."*

I became convinced the summer of 2000 qualified for the timing of this verse as well. All the computers continued to operate flawlessly after Y2K. The society let out a sigh of relief. Now that everything appears to be safe and back to normal, so I continued to expect the disaster to come suddenly.

But that summer came and went. The farmers began to reap the harvest, and I went back to the scriptures trying to understand, "How is it that it didn't happen?" My faith is strong that the scriptures are complete, and without exception every single verse and every single word will come to pass with impressive and perfect precision.

That's when I found in the Book of Daniel that Nebuchadnezzar's kingdom was attacked and taken away twelve months later from the time he was told that it would happen. We are told in 1 Corinthians 10:11 that all these stories from Israel's history are written down as examples for us on whom the end has come!

So, I though that possibly it will be like what happened to Nebuchadnezzar. I was actually relieved that it was going to happen twelve months later, and I was thankful because I had needed more time to prepare. But I continued in a sustained high degree of concern to warn everyone about what the Lord had shown me was going to happen.

THE WEEK OF THE ATTACK FORETOLD

In the fall of the year 2000, I came across a verse in Hosea 5:7, which says, *"They have dealt treacherously against the Lord, for they have borne illegitimate children. Now, the new moon will devour them with their land."*

I checked in another version, and it said, *"Devour them and their fields."* And still another version reads, *"...they've begotten pagan children."* I had recently seen a documentary on American college-age youth who were shaving their heads, covering themselves with tattoos—even including on their scalps. They were rampant with body piercing of lips, eyebrows, noses and tongues—all connected to pagan.

This is another confirming indictment in the scriptures that present-day society is performing with exact fulfillment of what was written thousands of years ago.

On the Day of the Lord the farmers will grieve because they have suffered the loss of their crops as Joel 1 previously explained. But a new moon is a reoccurring event each month. The moon makes a 28-day monthly cycle with four phases, each phase spanning seven days or one week.

Other scriptures have established this is going to happen in the middle of the night. The moon is the light that rules the night. The coming nuclear attack is going to be at night, during the phase of the new moon. We know the week because God's word tells us.

And Jesus said in Matthew 24, immediately following the Day of the Lord, *"The sun will be darkened, and the moon will not give its light."* Just like the sun is being darkened by smoke-filled skies, the full moon could conceivably be visible also through the haze of smoke-filled skies from cities burning. But we're told the moon does not give its light, and that fits the description during the phase of the new moon.

MYSTERIOUS SIGNS REVEALED TO ME

With great enthusiasm I devoured large portions of scriptures as the Lord continued to reveal marvelous mysteries hidden in his eternal word. I surmised that it is scripturally possible to know the timing of the sudden destruction called "the Day of the Lord" down to the week, because in Matthew

24, Jesus said that no man knows the day or the hour, but this attack will come in the middle of the night.

I began to understand this late in the year 2000, before the calendars for the next New Year were available. My curiosity grew as I wondered about how the timing of the new moon fit in relationship to the beginning of the next summer. As soon as I found a 2001 calendar, the first thing I did was look up the month of June to see what date the new moon fell on.

My eyes must have been twice their normal size as I stared at the date of June 21, on my new 2001 calendar. Above the large number "21" were the words "summer begins," and right below were the words "new moon" on the same date. I'm thinking what are the odds of this happening?

Accepting this as a confirming sign from the Lord, I did not need any further convincing. With a continuously sustained degree of urgency, I constantly tried to convince everyone that I knew the time of the end was at hand, and there was something we needed to do about it. And that was to stock up for the coming nuclear attack—followed up with the largest land invasion in the history of the world. This attack will result in a devastating crop contamination caused by radioactive fallout with a rippling effect that send the whole world into famine.

I returned to pursuing my profession in construction, motivated by the need to generate income to buy supplies and to be prepared. But the burden of the knowledge of what is going to happen so overwhelmed me one day while I was on the job that my arms became limp. I set my tools down, and I began to cry, "How can I keep working, while knowing that God has shown me what's coming—a sudden nuclear attack on American cities? Millions of lives are at stake. I must try to warn them."

MY FIRST TREK TO OUR NATION'S CAPITOL

Still overwhelmed with my newfound knowledge, I returned home, got on the Internet, and booked a round-trip flight from Reno to Washington, D.C. I intended to explain the details about these scriptures, and the parallels that exist between the scriptures and the current events and the remarkable timing of the 390 years of sin of the house of Israel. I needed to explain the relationship to the first English colony starting that long ago and the forty years of sin of the house of Judah with relationship to the transforming of American society in the 60's. Add to that the descriptions of the sinful behaviors taking place today that many years ago are what Ezekiel 8 predicted.

And so, that's how it came to be that I made my first trip to our nation's capitol. After I returned home from Washington, I found out there were crazy rumors going around in my hometown that I had been arrested for trying to break into the White House. The FBI had contacted the local sheriff's department in doing their standard check on my background.

My wife and family were upset with me. They felt humiliated by what I had done and what I was telling everyone. Also, it didn't sit well with the leadership of the church that I belonged to. Even though people doubted what I said, they still had to wait and see if I was right about what I said was going to happen.

One Sunday after church had been dismissed, I was telling some people who were visitors from out of town what I believed the Lord had shown me was going to happen. The pastor told the visitors, "No way does what Everett tell you represent this church" as he suddenly and rudely interrupted me. And again, in an angry manner, the pastor repeated what he had told me before..."I told you to stop talking about this on the church property. " The pastor had several times previously asked me not to talk on the church property about cities being destroyed by nuclear bombs. He said that I was scaring people, some of whom had stopped coming.

But I felt it was more important to obey God than to obey him for I had read in Ezekiel 3 that the watchman who doesn't warn the people would have their blood on his hands, and the Lord will hold him accountable for their lives. So I continued to tell everyone about the many scriptures that fit the description of the United States. Then one day when I was accused of trying to make everything fit, I told them, "When you go into a shoe store, you try to find a pair of shoes that fits. What do they say when you find shoes that fit? 'If the shoe fits, wear it.'"

On another occasion I was explaining some of the scriptures that pertain to this end-time destruction, and the pastor interrupted me and said, "That is just your opinion."

"Yes, it is," I agreed wholeheartedly. "And every Sunday morning, you stand in front of the whole congregation, read a passage of scripture, and then give your opinion about it."

I asked him, "Are you the only one in the whole church who is allowed to have an opinion?" He remained silent, unable to respond to my question. But these responses came instantly to me, and I later realized my spontaneous behavior fit the description of the watchman in Ezekiel 3 that says they are stubborn and obstinate, but I will make you even more stubborn and obstinate than the whole house of Israel.

I PERSISTED RELENTLESS IN MY EFFORTS

Then the summer of 2001 started, and what I had told everyone that was going to happen did not occur. Jesus said in Matthew 24 *"when summer is near it is at the door"* so I began to think maybe "at the door" means the door is about to be busted down anytime now. But I still could not relent from talking about the sudden disaster, it is still coming. And then at church I was told, "If you don't stop talking about it, we don't want you coming to church here anymore." You are frightening people and some have even stopped coming because of it." I later realized that there are some cowards even in the churches.

Revelations 21:8 tell us that the cowards will have their part in the lake of fire along with the murderers and liars and idolaters and fornicators. It becomes clear that all those forms of behavior are choices. You have a choice to be strong and courageous, or you can choose to be a coward. It is a clear choice—have faith, or let fear rule in your life.

Fear has torment, but God has not given to us a spirit of fear. But instead He gave us a spirit of power and of love and a sound mind. Perfect love casts out all fear. Cowards are to be despised for there is no place for them in God's kingdom. We are to choose to be strong and courageous for the Lord our God is with us and He will deliver us from all our enemies.

I said, "I've got news for you. I have never come to church because I thought that's what you wanted me to do. I come to church because it's what I want to do, and I still want to come, furthermore, I intend to continue to come as long as I want to."

Shortly thereafter one evening in July of 2001, the local sheriff's patrol car pulled up to my house, and a deputy came to the door and delivered a certified letter to me from the church. It said that the elders had all agreed that I was no longer considered a member of the church after twenty-nine years. And the letter said for me not to go there anymore. It was signed by the pastor and all the elders.

I thought, "This is a free country that was established by the shed blood of our founding forefathers to give us freedom of religion—to worship when and where we choose."

I felt strongly that if the day had come where people could be arrested simply for attending church, "Then let that day start here and now with me," I said. So I decided to go to church the very following Sunday morning.

ORDERED TO LEAVE THE CHURCH

I arrived at church that Sunday late during the services while the singing was nearly over. I sat down in a pew near the back row. As soon as he noticed that I was there, in front of the whole congregation, the pastor said over the microphone to me, "Everett, we told you not to come. Now if you don't leave, we're going to have to call the police."

I responded, "This is the Lord's house, and He doesn't tell anyone that they can't come. But you do what you think you've got to do." So the police were called, and the officer who arrived came in and sat down next to me in the pew at the rear of the church.

He said, "Everett, will you come outside and talk to me for a minute?"

"No," I explained, "I'm in the middle of a church service, and I don't appreciate being disturbed right now. When church is over, I'd be happy to talk with you and answer any questions you might have for the rest of the day."

So the deputy left, and a short while later he returned with the Chief of Police. Together, they both asked me if I would go outside with them, and again I said, "Not right now, I'm practicing my freedom of religion."

Then pastor came down and stood by them, and asked them, "Aren't you going to arrest him?"

They said, "No. He's not doing anything wrong. So, we can't arrest him."

Then, the pastor said, "Well, I'm going to make a citizens arrest."

"For what?" the puzzled officers asked.

"For trespassing—I told him not to come in here, and he did anyway."

And so the officers said, "Okay, Everett, stand up. You're under arrest." They put handcuffs on me and took me to jail.

DEPUTIES THREW ME IN JAIL

After being fingerprinted and booked, deputies put me in a booking cell. I was the only one in the cold and clammy room. After a while I laid down on this pathetic plastic mat, buried my head in my arm, covered up my eyes, and began to pray, "Lord, why are these things happening to me? I don't understand what is going on. All I wanted to do was continue attending church and share the things that the Lord was showing me."

Then it occurred to me, "You're being charged with trespassing." Immediately, the Lord's Prayer came to mind.

"Father, forgive us our trespasses, as we forgive those who trespass against us."

I thought, well, if I have trespassed against them, they certainly are not forgiving me. I then shuttered at the thought of their predicament, that being of their trespasses not being forgiven them.

After being released on $300 bail, I went home, prayerfully seeking the Lord about why these strange trials were coming upon me. I got my Bible out to read it. And that very day upon opening it, I discovered the verse in Hosea 9:8, which says about the watchman: "Snares await him in all his paths, and hostility in the house of his God."

All I wanted was to talk about what the Bible says at church. For that I was handcuffed and taken to jail? You might expect that kind of reaction at a tavern or bar, but church is supposed to be where you can go to talk about the Bible. What has happened to me is certainly finding hostility in the house of God. The cold hard fact is that the Lord God Almighty himself has without a doubt called me to be a watchman. Again, strangely enough God's word contains information that is beyond coincidence and appropriately applies exactly to my situation in an astoundingly accurate and timely manner. The Lord had again provided me with consolation and confirmation.

"THE WHOLE HOUSE OF ISRAEL IS HARDENED AND OBSTINATE"

One day, I read to a friend of mine the verses about the watchman in Ezekiel 3 that says, *Son of man, go now to the House of Israel and speak my words to them, but the house of Israel is not willing to listen to you, because they're not willing to listen to me—for the whole house of Israel is hardened and obstinate.*

"But I will make you as unyielding and hardened as they are. I will make your forehead like the hardest stone, harder than flint."

After I read that verse to my friend, he said, "The Lord must have known what he was doing, when he chose you. You are without a doubt the most stubborn and the hardest-headed person I know."

Over and over, the scriptures describe things that happened to me and what has occurred in my life. I found myself daily telling people about what has happened to me as far as slipping off of the roof and breaking my left arm and left leg. And then, I tell them how I came home from the hospital, and opened the Bible to the verse in Ezekiel 4 that says, *"As for you, lie down on your left side."*

As I began to tell them, I would unbutton and roll up the sleeve of my shirt to show them the scars that remain on my arm from where the fractured and splintered bone came out and the holes made by the bolts from orthopedic surgery. I had been doing this repeatedly and then one day as I was reading over the same passages in Ezekiel that I had read many times before, I suddenly realized that Ezekiel 4:7 says, *"With bared arm prophesy against them."*

I thought "Hey, that's exactly what I have been doing without even thinking about it; and here are the instructions telling the watchman to do just that!"

I had just stepped up onto a newly installed colored metal roof when suddenly my foot slipped and down I fell. That is described in Deuteronomy 32:35. *"In due time their foot will slip; their day of disaster is near; their doom rushes upon them."* The preceding context verses 20 & 29 say what their end will be; the four judgments of Ezekiel 14 sword-famine-plague-wild beasts are in verses 24 & 25; and consistent will end time judgment verse 32 has the link to Sodom and Gomorrah.

Finding the scriptures verses that describe what I am already doing on a daily basis has only continued to convince me even more so, that who I am is the watchman sent to this generation. So I remain compelled to warn of this impending disaster to all who will listen, for I have wept at the thought of anyone's blood on my hands.

GOD'S WORD REMAINS IN MY HEART LIKE A BURNING FIRE

Every year since 1999, the Lord has revealed to me abundant evidence and signs of the coming end-time that marks the beginning of a new era. In the process, predictions made by Jeremiah in the Old Testament have come true to me. As Jeremiah stated, *I've been ridiculed all day long, and everyone mocks me whenever I speak.* Even so, just as he foretold, I cry out "claiming violence and destruction."

So, conveying the Word of the Lord has at times brought me insult and reproach. All day long I cannot avoid mentioning Him or speaking more in His name. His Word is in my heart like a burning fire. I'm unable to hold these details within me for to do so makes me feel weary.

For me to face ridicule and rejection is not hard because with the Lord and the truths that have been revealed to me I am overwhelmed and glad in my heart.

Although well liked throughout my community, when I enter a crowded room, some people now ignore me or walk away. They know what the main topic of my conversation is. I tell everyone about this coming day of destruction, and they don't particularly care to hear about it. Even among groups of close friends, they will say to each other, "Please don't get him started". There are people used to say, "Hey, Everett! It's good to see you, and how have you been doing," but now when they see me they just look the other way.

Faced with such rejection, at times I'm guilty of failing to follow the Bible's instructions for the watchman: *"Let them refuse who refuse; let them listen who will listen."* Ezekiel says, *"Whoever will refuse, let them refuse for they are a rebellious house."*

I've had a difficult time trying to be obedient to that particular scripture. Essentially, this means that if people don't listen, in those instances I need to just give it up and walk away. That is hard for me to do. Yet I have an overwhelming desire to find someone who cares to hear the truth. And there are some of those who do listen and tell me that they greatly appreciate the insight that I share with them. Those who love the truth and recognize it when they hear it are a source of great joy to me. There is great comfort knowing all my efforts are not in vain. Some have taken action and began to acquire quantities of essential supplies. Many are caused to seek the Lord, for whom else can we turn to in this coming time of distress?

REPENT AND LIVE

Here we can cherish the promise of a new world coming, like heaven on earth as in the Lord's Prayer, *"Thy kingdom come, thy will be done, here on earth as it is in heaven."* This is a loving place enjoyed by those who are righteous. This is the way the meek shall inherit the earth, while souls of sinners die.

But since the Bible urges us to be righteous, how do we know what that is? The Holy Book continually defines this as avoiding of sins by paying attention to and keeping God's laws, such as the Ten Commandments, while also loving our neighbors as ourselves.

On numerous occasions, and in various chapters, Ezekiel repeatedly warns us that the "soul who sins is the one who will die." In 18:30, he warns us to "turn away from all your offenses; sin will not be your downfall.

"Rid yourself of the offenses you have committed. Get a new heart and a new spirit." Driving the point home, the Lord says, *"Why will you die, oh house of Israel, for I take no pleasure in the death of anyone—declares the sovereign Lord. Repent and live."*

CHAPTER 10

"THEY ASKED JESUS TO SHOW THEM A SIGN"

The last night of my trip to Washington, D.C., I awakened in my hotel room at two o'clock in the morning. There was an eerie stillness about the room. I thought it strange and suspected that the Lord had awakened me. So, I picked up the Bible and opened it to see if the Lord might show me something significant. Where I began to read was Matthew 16:2-4: They asked Jesus to show them a sign. He said, *"When evening comes, you say, 'It will be fair weather, for the sky is red.' And in the morning, 'Today it will be stormy because the sky is red and overcast.' You know how to interpret the appearance of the sky, but you cannot interpret the signs of the times. A wicked and adulterous generation looks for a miraculous sign, but none will be given it except the sign of Jonah.*

Jesus then left them and went away." I thought about this present day and age, and today it is a wicked and adulterous generation. People I've talked to have said to me, "I have to see a sign."

Jesus is saying that although they are looking for a sign at the time of the end, *"no sign will be given to them, except the sign of Jonah.* We need to focus on that exception, because it is the only sign that they will be given."* They are the generation who this end time destruction comes on. So there is going to be a sign given to them after all. And it is the sign of Jonah. I began to think about what that could possibly mean, because it has got to be out there for all to see.

Well, in construction, building codes also have exceptions, and I have learned to pay careful attention to them. Also many county ordinances like planning and zoning laws have numerous exceptions. It is always a good idea to pay careful attention to all those exceptions as well.

AM I THE SIGN OF JONAH?

So, I thought a great deal about Jonah. He was an ordinary man whom the Lord told to go preach repentance to the capitol city of Nineveh because of its wickedness. Bear in mind that while I am reading this, I am in our capitol city of Washington, D.C. trying to warn all the high ranking elected officials there as well.

But Jonah tried to run away, and he got aboard a ship—and a violent storm arose. The ship was threatened, and the sailors were afraid. They found out that Jonah was responsible. So, he told them to throw him into the sea, and that it would become calm.

And when they threw him overboard, the raging sea became calm. Then all the sailors greatly feared the Lord. But then the Lord provided a great fish to swallow Jonah and he was inside the fish for three days and three nights. When he began to pray from inside the belly of a whale, the Lord commanded the fish to vomit Jonah onto dry land. It was then that Jonah decided to obey the word of the Lord, and he went to the very large city of Nineveh and preached to them for three days—like he was supposed to from the beginning.

No doubt, Jonah's three days in the belly of the whale altered his physical appearance. Some say his skin would have been bleached completely white by the stomach acid of the whale. At any rate, if a man comes to you and tells you that he just spent three days in the belly of a whale, and the only reason he's standing before you is because God delivered him out of the belly of the whale so he could tell you to repent—well, that's a whale of a fish story.

COMPARE MY STORY TO JONAH'S

But the story I tell about all that has happened to me is no less strange than what happened to Jonah. And I bear scars that physically reflect the reality of my story.

Like telling people how I slipped and fell and suffered a badly broken left wrist and left ankle, and then came home and opened a bible to "As for you lie down on your left side." plus I roll up the sleeve of my shirt and show them the scar where a sharp bone fragment came out and then one day as I was rereading Ezekiel Chapter 4 "...with bared arm prophecy to them." Once again a feeling of awe swept over me. Who am I?

When you recount the series of strange things that have happened to me and all the stories in this book, I'm convinced that Jonah's story is no stranger than mine.

SIGNS ARE EVERYWHERE. Failure to pay attention to these signs can cost you your life.

Can it be that no sign will be given to them except me? How else can I explain all these things that have happened to me?

I returned to my hometown and summer passed by without the biblical disaster called the Day of the Lord. Again I'm at a loss for an explanation to why we seem to have escaped the sudden end-time disaster in 2001.

A HARD LOOK AT TOBACCO

So I began to re-read the history of Jamestown. And I discovered that it was really in 1612 that they actually learned how to grow and cure tobacco. And tobacco is totally credited with having saved the colony from becoming a wretched failure.

Tobacco transformed the colony into a raging boomtown. Immediately I recognized tobacco as sin, for the Bible tells us, "The wages of sin is death." And we know tobacco kills people. But sin is also described in another place, that "whatever you yield yourself to, that you will become enslaved by." Whoever yields to smoking becomes enslaved by one of the most powerful addictions known to man. It is said that heroin addiction is more easily broken than an addiction to tobacco.

EZEKIEL WITNESSED MEN SMOKING TOBACCO PIPES

So, I began to add 390 years to 1612, and I became convinced that it would happen the next year in 2002. My conviction was re-enforced when I was re-reading in the Book of Ezekiel, and I discovered scriptures that actually fit the description of smoking tobacco. Ezekiel is told to go see the wicked, detestable things they are doing.

So, he went and looked, and he saw in this room seventy elders of the House of Israel. We've already been told they'll be punished 390 days, a day for each year of their sins. Each one of them is holding in his hand a censer.

How do you describe a censer? It's a small fire resistant container, designed for holding a smoldering substance. Out of it, rises a wisp of smoke. Ezekiel also sees a cloud of incense in the room rising above them. Tobacco smoking began with pipes, and they are commonly held in the hand. But today a censer that has incense in it is more likely to be set down somewhere and the small amount of smoke from it dissipates rather than forming a cloud. The evolvement of cigars and cigarettes came later.

A roomful of men smoking pipes will create a cloud of smoke in the air. I began to recognize the beginning of their sin, and it is tobacco.

Add 390 to 1612 and you get 2002. Isaiah 29:1 says add year to year, so now I am convinced of the need to continue to prepare for the next year and rejoice in fact that God has apparently given us an extension of more time.

THE BIBLICAL PUZZLE

I see each Bible verse like a piece of a puzzle. And I see one fitting into another one in the same way that if you have the wrong piece of the puzzle, it may appear that it fits into an adjoining piece. But as the other puzzle pieces begin to fill in around it, it'll become obvious that piece doesn't belong there.

The Bible says we know in part, and I know the Lord has given me a large part of what I see coming. It's a cleansing of our land. I tell people that I know what is going to happen. I'm not a rocket scientist. I just read about it in God's Word.

In II Peter 2, it says, "The Lord condemned the cities of Sodom and Gomorrah by burning them to ashes, and he made them an example of what is going to happen to the ungodly." At first, I had trouble with this verse. How can a city suffer nuclear devastation but only the ungodly suffer exclusively?

Right after Jeremiah 6 reiterates terrible destruction from the north (linking this to Ezekiel 7:5's unique end-time coming disaster; and that being in Ezekiel 1:4 the immense fire cloud enfolding itself and coming from the north.) He tells us that they plan to attack at noon. But alas, the daylight fades, and the shadows grow long, indicating possibly that they will have trouble logistically getting everything into place on time. If so, they are forced to make a last-minute change of plans and then decide to make it an attack at night.

But it's God's mercy on the righteous that their intended plans are delayed. For the city is a crowded place at noon, and the population is near peak levels when they planned to attack.. The devastation and human casualties would be much greater then, but because it happens in the middle of the night, when the typical city experiences the lowest levels of population in a twenty-four hour cycle during the wee hours of the morning. There is a lingering element of society that continues to mill about, looking for drugs, sex, and other criminal activity. And it is upon their heads this disaster will suddenly fall.

9/11 ATTACK ON AMERICA

On September 11, 2001, I got up and went to work, and I was unaware of what was taking place till I stopped at a convenience store to get a drink. The man I met coming out of the door of the store said, "I bow down before you." He was a friend who I had discussed at great length how convinced I was that we were facing the end-time disaster. I told him, "I don't want anyone to bow down before me. What are you talking about?"

He said, "You were right. Haven't you heard?"

"Heard what?" I asked. "I haven't heard anything."

He then informed me.

I told him that this was not the Day of the Lord disaster that is coming. But I did recognize it to be like a contraction in the birth pain process. The Day of the Lord is coming, and it'll be like the breaking of the water. When the water breaks the pains greatly increase. That will be the actual beginning of the baby passing through the birth canal. It is then that the pain becomes exceedingly great.

"BIRTH PAINS" SIGNAL THE END OF THIS AGE

When Jesus sat on Mount Olive in Matthew Chapter 24, the disciples asked him when the end of age would come.

The Lord answered when we see wars, rumors of wars, nation rising against nation, kingdoms rising against kingdoms, famines, and earthquakes this will be the beginning of birth pains.

The Earth is groaning in travail. The contractions have begun. There is no reverse. The process has no timeouts. Painful events shall continue and become even more severe.

Recent key events in this process included the Bush-Gore election, the attacks of 9-11 in New York City, the war on terror, our attack on Iraq, the horrific tsunami in Southeast Asia, and Hurricane Katrina in New Orleans, Hurricane Rita, and the whole Gulf Coast—called the worst disaster in the history of the United States. These are followed by the worst tornado season; wild fires fifty times more severe than the average, and floods and severe droughts.

These birth pains are the necessary process that results in the birthing of the "NEW AGE." There is coming incredible period of economic and technological expansion far exceeding what followed World War II. We will emerge as the champions of this final conflict, and there will be peace on earth for a thousand years to come.

First Thessalonians 5:2 says that while people speak of peace and safety, destruction will come upon them suddenly as if labor pains suffered by a woman. In fact, anywhere labor pains are mentioned throughout the Bible, all such references refer to this transition-time.

Birth pain, although an unpleasant process, is the way that new life is produced. And the new age is being slowly birthed as war intensifies until all the evil enemies of freedom are completely destroyed..WITH THE LORD'S HELP WILL EMERGE VICTORIOUS.

Thus, for brief intermittent periods, life throughout American society will appear to return to normal while in fact the end-time birth pain contraction process continues to escalate.

THE BEST TIME FOR AN ATTACK

But the Lord confirmed my understanding about this later as I watched a couple of retired generals being interviewed on a talk show. They were asked, "When do you think the Bush administration will attack Iraq?"

By this time, officials had announced their plans to do so in advance. That didn't seem particularly prudent, from my point of view, to make an announcement that you're coming to attack your enemy. But nevertheless, one general responded to the question by saying, "With today's technology and equipment, the optimum time for an attack is in the middle of the night, because the darkness helps maintain the element of surprise. With our night vision goggles, we have an advantage.

"The cover of darkness keeps our enemies from seeing us coming," the general said. "The darker it is the better, and the darkest nights are during the phase of the new moon."

Again I am amazed at how the Lord confirms to me that the understanding I have is supported by scripture and present day logic of military experts..

This is what the Bible is talking about. Another scripture that verifies what the Lord has shown me is in Genesis, Chapter 1. It says, *"The Lord made the lights in the sky to separate the night from the day. God said, 'Let there be light in the sky to separate the night from the day, and let them serve as SIGNS, and to mark seasons, and days, and years.'"*

It's easy to understand that the sun marks the day. And the seasons are caused by the tilt of the earth. We revolve around the sun once each year. But when it says, they serve as a signs it's telling us that the sun and the moon both serve as indicators

of timing references to when this climactic end-time disaster of
all disasters will come.

ONE FOURTH OF THE EARTH—-NORTH AMERICA
The scriptures are clear that this coming disaster doesn't
refer to the entire earth. The primary reasons:

1 SEASONS: Since the disaster is at the door as summer
approaches, it can only happen only in one hemisphere—either
the north half or the south half. When it's summer in the United
States, it's winter in South America.

2 NIGHTTIME ATTACKS: As the earth turns on its axis,
no more than half of it is experiencing the darkness of night
time at the same time; but nighttime is continuously moving.

One-half times one-half equals one-fourth, and that
explains why the four horsemen of Revelations Chapter Six are
given power to kill by sword, famine, plague, and wild beasts
over ONE FOURTH OF THE EARTH.

By continuing to seek out the specific descriptions
pertaining to the "day of the Lord" you will become convinced
exactly which ONE FOURTH OF THE EARTH is awaiting
this destruction.

The Day of the Lord

COMES LIKE A THIEF IN THE NIGHT, WHEN SUMMER IS NEAR, FARMERS GRIEVE OVER THE LOSS OF WHEAT& BARLEY, THE LORD TAKES AWAY THE HARVEST.

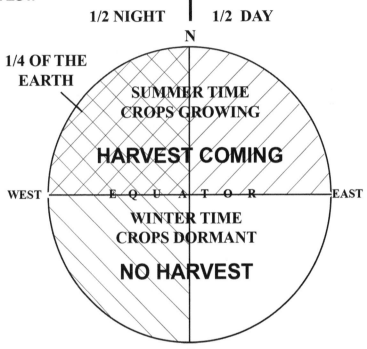

1/2 NIGHT | 1/2 DAY

N

1/4 OF THE EARTH

SUMMER TIME
CROPS GROWING

HARVEST COMING

WEST — E Q U A T O R — EAST

WINTER TIME
CROPS DORMANT

NO HARVEST

S

THE FOUR HORSEMEN ARE GIVEN POWER TO KILL OVER

ONE FOURTH THE EARTH

BY SWORD FAMINE, PLAGUE & WILD BEASTS
REVELATION 6:8

"WHAT IS GOING TO HAPPEN (TO THE UNGODLY)"

2 Peter 2 says what happened to Sodom and Gomorrah is an example of what's going to happen to the ungodly.

So, anyone who wants to know what is going to happen should take a very close look at how that story unfolded. I have encountered many who tell me that they are happy and don't even really want to know what is going to happen.

First, the city was wicked, and Lot was told by the angel to, *"Get out because God is going to destroy this city."* And the Lord sent an angel to get Lot to obey this, he narrowly escaped and survived, but his wife perished.

Today, the Lord is warning people to get out of the cities. Major cities are the target for the coming attack. People need to understand this for what it is: an example of the coming Day of the Lord; cities will be burned; in the middle of the night. Do not remain in the metropolitan areas after the sun goes down. If they obey, they will increase their chances of survival. Now, the angel told Lot to go up into the mountains, just like in Ezekiel Chapter 7, which says, "All who survive and escape will be in the mountains."

But Lot protested, "Why do I need to go there? There's nothing there." He pleaded with the angel, and said, "Why can't I just go to this nearby small town instead?" The angel conceded, and said to him, "Okay, go ahead and go into the nearby small town." But very soon, because of the violence in the nearby small town, Lot began to fear for his life. This is just like what Ezekiel 7 informs us, that those in the country—which is like a nearby small town—will die by the sword. Those who remain in the city will perish by famine and plague.

Next, we read about Lot doing what he was told to do to start with. He left that small town full of violence and went up into the mountains, and stayed in a cave where he was safe. This also serves as a good example to follow as the need arises at the appropriate time. Caves make excellent fallout shelters and even in Isaiah 2 we read about the men fleeing to the caves and holes in the ground from the fear and dread of the Lord. Lot is providing us with another example of what to do on the Day of the Lord.

NUCLEAR ATTACKS HIT BIG CITIES

Major U.S. cities will be the direct target on the Day of the Lord. America's enemies want to kill as many people as possible. Isaiah 1 says cities will be burned and Ezekiel 5 says, *"...the fire will burn in the center of the city."*

Isaiah 20:8 tells us *"The Lord will be a spirit of justice, to him who sits in judgments, a source of strength to those who turn back the battle at the gate."*

The word "gate" here applies to the entrances of the country—specifically the United States. Our nation's founders made use of this word.

For instance, New York City on the East Coast is called "The Gateway to Freedom," and San Francisco on the West Coast is the gateway to the "Golden State" and has the famed Golden Gate Bridge.

Such port cities are major entrances to our nation, like New Orleans, which just suffered the worst natural disaster our nation's history. New Orleans also serves as an example of what is coming. Prudent men see how quickly disaster can strike. I like to be optimistic and hope for the best, but preparing for worst-case scenario is wise. Isaiah 31 says the noble man makes noble plans and by noble deeds he stands. Will you be able to stand on the day of the Lord's wrath? Yes you will, if you get busy and make your own noble plans.

A "Sodom and Gomorrah" mentality is prevalent in today's major cities. But people who prefer to avoid the oppressive congestion there live in the country or the mountains and enjoy the tranquility from being closer to God's creation. Those who desire the nightlife and party action seek out the city lights will risk suffering the coming destruction.

THE CITIES HAVE BECOME OUR FALSE GODS

Jeremiah 11:13 says, *"The number of your cities are the number of your gods."* Architectural masterpieces form the city skyline competing for recognition. City planners pride themselves with elaborate designed transit systems, flood control and utility networks. Our society places prestige from money and materialism above all else, worshipping them. The Old Testament terminology refers to this as idolatry.

Indeed, real estate prices within our largest cities and the areas surrounding them have reached staggering levels. The Bible tells us that the love of money is the root of all evil.

The greed mentality has stricken many of those areas, but that same mentality is spreading.

PAY ATTENTION TO ALL THE EXAMPLES
Many other stories in the scriptures also serve us as examples to us. They confirm that all the stories in Israel's history are written down for us upon whom the end will come just like we are told in 1 Corinthians 10:11.

I discovered everywhere I found passages referring to what happened to Sodom and Gomorrah that it was consistently foretelling of the same unique end-time disaster.

One such verse is in Deuteronomy 29:23, and another one is in Isaiah 1:9.

Isaiah chapter 1 talks about a sinful nation, a brood of evildoers, children given to corruption. They have forsaken the Lord; they have spurned the holy one, and turned their backs on him.

"Why should you be beaten anymore? Why do you persist in rebellion? Your whole head is injured." Think of 9-11.

As the miles and miles of destruction by Hurricane Katrina of the Mississippi coast were shown on television from the air as cameramen flew over, the Governor of Mississippi, Haley Barbour, made the comment that they took a blow on the jaw. He added that they would recover. How's that for fulfillment of the scripture "Why should you be beaten anymore?" It is because America will not listen or wake up to the fact that God is doing everything He can to get us to turn around and repent.

"Your whole heart is afflicted," which we can think of Hurricane Katrina and New Orleans. The port of New Orleans was the heart of the shipping into the interior of our land. The Mississippi River is like the aorta distributing needed supplies into the heartland.

It says in Amos 3:6, if a disaster comes upon a city, "...*has not the Lord caused it?*" Without a doubt it is the Lord who has caused the United States to suffer this worst hurricane season ever. Even insurance companies refer to such disasters as "acts of God".

Isaiah 1:9 says that "*Unless the Lord left us some survivors, we would have become like Sodom, and we would have been like Gomorrah.*"

Because this verse is talking about Sodom and Gomorrah, we know that this entire context is talking about what is going to happen to the ungodly. And it is all end time prophetic information. It's preceded by:

"*Your country is desolate, your cities burned with fire.*"

Isaiah 2 continues with the Day of the Lord, saying "*men will flee to caves in the rocks and holes in the ground.*"

Now, that's a typical response to a radiation-contaminated environment. Isaiah 3 says, "*The Lord is about to take supply and support, all supplies of food and all supplies of water.*"

This is just like at the end of Ezekiel 4, where we learn that "*food and water will be scarce.*"

This refers to the Day of the Lord, and Joel 1 says, "*Even the flocks of sheep are suffering. And the cattle moan because they have no pasture.*"

Why is that? The environment is experiencing a nuclear winter. Hope lies in the fact that spring will come again. Can you make it through the winter?

And then we get to the part in Isaiah 3:9 where they parade their sin like Sodom. We do have gay pride parades in these times as I have already told about seeing them on the news on the first day I had read this verse for the first time. But please don't forget the next verse that promises it will be well for the righteous, they will enjoy the fruit of their deeds or doings or actions, depending upon which version you have. Just so you get the point that this is a time that calls for the righteous to be busy doing deeds and taking action. What they are to be doing is preparing to deal with what we are told is coming.

THE PHARAOH SERVES AS ONE EXAMPLE

In October 2000 I went down to Guatemala. While on the way there, I was thinking about the story of the Pharaoh, and how he had dreamt of seven fat cows that were consumed by seven skinny cows. And he awakened from that dream, and he paced the floor troubled by how unusual the dream was. He knew it must mean something significant, but he didn't understand it.

So, he lay down again, and went back to sleep and dreamt again. He dreamt about seven abundant stocks of grain that were consumed by seven drought-stricken, sickly looking stocks of grain.

The Pharaoh awakened from the dream and recognized the significance of the similarity of these dreams. When he sought far and wide for someone to interpret them, along came Joseph who explained to the Pharaoh that the dreams meant that seven years of famine was coming.

But they would be preceded by seven abundant years. The Pharaoh put Joseph in charge of stockpiling grain in preparation of seven years of famine to come. I thought about the future seven years of tribulation coming, described as seven years of famine—where it'll be a day's wages for a quart of wheat, according to Revelation 6:5.

Late at night as I lay in the strange bed trying to go to sleep, I thought about Ezekiel's instructions in Chapter 4, that say to store up for yourself wheat, barley, and beans. Because of the seven years of coming tribulation, I began to suspect that the story of Pharaoh's Egypt was another example for those of us upon whom the end will come. This is an important discovery. The Lord often reveals an important message by using similar, but different stories. Like in the Pharaoh's two different dreams, they were both about the same message. This is consistent with what I am saying about many Old Testament stories. They are different but similar examples about that same future event, the "Day of the Lord". The Pharaoh lies down a second time after the first dream similar to Ezekiel who also lies down a second time on his right side. The parallels in both stories serve as evidence that these and other stories are in fact examples given to us to help us understand what is going to happen.

At six o'clock the next morning, I was in a men's shower room shampooing my head with my eyes closed. And my thoughts were about the Pharaoh and the seven fat cows and seven skinny cows and wondering whether it also was an example to us. When I stepped out of the shower with a towel around my waist, one of three men at the other end of the shower room saw me step out of the shower and said to his friends, "Hey, look at him. He has one fat leg, and one skinny leg."

It was true. My broken leg had shriveled up and shrunken from muscle atrophy. The good leg had been carrying the full load of my weight, and the muscle had gotten bigger from the continuous workout. I told them right then what I had been thinking and that the Lord was speaking to me through what they had just said.

And I told them, "Just like in the time of the Egyptian Pharaoh who enslaved the Israelites and God saw the heavy burden of His people, He was moved with compassion and delivered them, so it is the same today, God's people struggle under the heavy oppression of this corrupt and wicked system of diminished Liberty and Justice. This is supposed to be "THE LAND OF THE FREE; THE HOME OF THE BRAVE" but I fear it has become more like "THE LAND OF THE FEE; HOME OF THE SLAVE."

So another sign of the time of the end drawing near will be seven years of unprecedented economic expansion, then the year that the sudden destruction comes and that begins the seven years of tribulation."

I had watched an economic news program saying that during the Clinton administration the country had experienced a continuous, unprecedented economic expansion for the last seven years.

So, I added that to my logical basis for being convinced that we were now at the end of seven abundant years, and that the seven years of tribulation were due to begin. With these compelling facts supporting what I already knew, I continued to tell everyone to get ready for the coming Day of Disaster.

CHAPTER 11

THE UNITED STATES ABANDONS THE ABM TREATY

After the terrorist attack of Sept. 11, 2001, the Bush administration announced that a missile defense system was needed to protect our country, and that they were going to make it a top priority. But we were still party to the ABM Treaty with Russia that said we could not put up a missile defense system.

The peace had been maintained by what was called "mutually assured destruction." Successfully putting into place a missile defense system would upset Russia's balance of power. We could still potentially destroy them, but they could not do anything about it.

President Bush tried to persuade Russian leader Mr. Putin to mutually consent to abandon the treaty. But President Putin responded by saying, *"The treaty is the hinge pin on which world peace and stability revolves, and it should remain in effect as it is."* President Bush explained to Mr. Putin that with or with out his consent, the United States was not going to continue to be subject to the ABM Treaty.

President Bush then gave the six months written notification to Russia that the United States was going to withdraw from the treaty as was required in that agreement. In an interview Mr. Putin was told that the notification to withdraw had been given, and they asked for his response. All he said was:

"Mr. Bush makes a mistake."

The notification to withdraw from the treaty was given in mid-December of 2001, meaning that the actual point in time that the treaty would become null and void would be June 15, 2002.

That's the time of the year when "summer is near." It fits the time frame given in Matthew 24:32, for the coming attack known as the day of the Lord. I thought, "Well, we broke the treaty with Russia. They can justify attacking us. After all, they wanted to keep the treaty, but we broke it."

Again I am overwhelmingly convinced that the Lord is showing me all these signs and confirming to me what is going to happen near the middle of the year to come. I feel the pressure of knowing what is going to happen and feel responsible to try to warn everyone about it, and that I will be held accountable if I don't warn them.

THE TREATY IS BROKEN

As I continued studying scriptures, I had read Chapter 33 of Isaiah several times in various translations without noticing one particular statement that it made. But the talk on the news about the ABM Treaty suddenly made a powerfully appropriate verse—that I had failed to previously notice—jump out at me.

It says, *"The treaty is broken, the cities are despised, no one is respected. The land mourns and wastes away.... People are burned to lime."*

Again, I had no difficulty relating these scriptures to nuclear devastation, and the treaty that it says is broken, I instantly knew to be none other than the ABM Treaty.

On Christmas morning of 2001, I opened a present from my sixteen-year-old daughter, and it was a book about President Ronald Reagan.

It contained historic information that gave me clear insight about Russia. When I picked up the book, it opened right to the page where it tells about how Russian leader Mikhail Gorbachev was upset about Reagan's plan to pursue the Star Wars missile defense system.

Gorbachev said, *"How do I know once you put your missile defense system in place that you won't use it as a shield, from which to launch a pre-emptive strike?"*

President Reagan tried to convince him that the United States was a peaceful nation. But Gorbachev said, *"You say your intentions are peaceful. But I can't gamble the security of the Soviet people on your say-so. I cannot let you build it."* They left that meeting with unresolved conflict. Reagan never got it built, and the following administrations of Bush and Clinton made little progress on it.

It has now become a top priority since 9/11, and Russian leader Putin must view our new missile Defense system just like Gorbachev did.

He may not be saying it; but just like Gorbachev said, he cannot let us build it. Russia is not our friend, and they do not trust us any more today than they did back then.

We have enjoyed world peace based on mutually assured destruction. It is called a Mexican standoff—a cocked and loaded gun held to each other's head, a no win situation. But our building the new missile defense system is like taking the firing pin out of their gun. As we near it's completion their window of opportunity to stop us is closing. If they are ever going to try to stop us, it has to be soon.

I would not know how nor have I tried to seek out this type of information. But when it is suddenly in front of me I have no doubt but the Lord is equipping me with insight and understanding.

I continued to stress the warning about what I saw coming to all those I came in contact with.

CHAPTER 12

JOB SUFFERED SO WE CAN UNDERSTAND WHAT IS COMING

I began to see other stories in the Old Testament that have striking similarities, paralleling what I envision coming upon us.

Take Job, for example. He was a righteous and prosperous man. But all in the same day, like the Day of the Lord, he was suddenly attacked by enemies, Sabeans and three bands of Chaldeans, who ran off with his livestock and killed his servants.

A big ball of fire fell from the sky, and burned up his livestock and killed his servants. And suddenly a mighty wind swept in from the desert, and struck all four corners of the house killing his children that were in it. And the house was completely blown away. It reminded me of the documentary I watched of the atomic bomb, and the buildings that were shown as the blast disintegrated all four corners of them.

Then, Job is seen sitting in a pile of ashes, like fallout dust. There's baldness on his head, like hair loss from radiation. And he's scraping sores and boils from the soles of his feet to the top of his head, similar to what radiation sickness would be like.

The New Testament tells us we're to remember Job, that the Lord is merciful and full of grace. Why is that?

It's because during the coming tribulation, many godly men may experience trials just as severe as Job, but we're reminded to remember Job because the Lord is merciful and restored everything back to him and gave him double what he had before.

1 Corinthians 10 says that Israel's history is written down as examples for us upon whom the end will come. The more I thought about what this verse says, the more I realized how incredible God is. He orchestrated all the events in Israel's history to depict specifically for this end-time generation examples of what is going to happen.

Job makes an excellent example for us to follow when the end time trials come upon us.

When he lost everything, he said, "...*blessed be the name of the Lord. Naked I came from my mother's womb and naked to the grave I will go. The Lord giveth and the Lord taketh away.*"

When he was afflicted unto death, he said, "...*though He slay me yet will I serve Him.*" He understood what it is like to belong to the Lord. If we belong to the Lord it is because He purchased us at cavalry, by the blood He shed for our sin. He has every right to do with us as He chooses. Because He promises to, we know that He will give us strength to endure whatever He requires of us.

Isaiah 61 verifies this saying they will rebuild the ancient ruins and restore the places long devastated. It says, "*They will inherit a double portion in their land, and everlasting joy will be theirs.*"

We will recover and rebuild the cities in the same way that Hiroshima and Nagasaki have been rebuilt. We can look forward to a coming time of world peace, a rapidly expanding economy, when there will be double prosperity compared to what we have today, for the Lord is coming to establish His kingdom and dwell among us (Zechariah 2).

THE KING"S DREAM REVEALS OUR FUTURE

In Chapter 4 of the book of Daniel, It begins with a dream that King Nebuchadnezzar had about a great tree whose height was enormous. The tree grew large and strong, and its top touched to the sky. It was visible to the ends of the earth.

Its leaves were beautiful, its fruits were abundant and on it were fruits for all. From it, every creature was fed. The description is a perfect example of this great nation.

We are referred to as the breadbasket of the world, because we produce huge surpluses of corn and grain for export. Our large economy is the envy of the whole world. We have achieved enormous heights economically, politically and militarily. Militarily we are so strong that we are called the sole remaining super power. Our dominion extends to the distant parts of the earth. We have military bases all over the world.

After the European conflict had ended, Hiroshima and Nagasaki had been nuked, and WWII was coming to an end, the Admiral of the United States Navy was asked, "What do you see as the mission of the United States Navy now?"

He responded, "We will continue to patrol and control all seven seas of the world. The international waters cover more than two thirds of the earth's surface, and we have been solely in control of it since World War II." No one has been able to challenge us. But the challenge is coming. Evidence that our dominion extends to the distant parts of the earth is all around us.

I believe this dream to be prophetic and about the kingdom of the United States. The seven years of coming tribulation is depicted. We supply the whole world with food. We have satellites in the heavens, like the top of the tree that touches the sky. Our navy patrols and controls all seven seas of the world since WWII.

The dream made the king afraid, and he called for his wise men to come and interpret it for him. Daniel told the king that the dream represented him and his kingdom for his greatness had grown and become strong, reached unto heaven, and had dominion to the ends of the earth.

Daniel interprets the dream for the king, saying that a decree has been issued against the king and his kingdom: *"You will be driven away from people and live with the wild animals, and eat grass like cattle and be drenched with the dew of heaven. Seven times will pass by you, until you acknowledge that the most high is sovereign over the kingdoms of men—and gives them to anyone he wishes."*

"The command to leave the stump of the tree with its roots means that your kingdom will be restored to you. Therefore, please accept my advice. Renounce your sins by doing what is right, and be kind to the oppressed. Then, your prosperity will continue."

Excellent advice for America today would be the same—renounce our sins by doing what is right, and be kind to the oppressed. Then America's prosperity would continue.

We can be assured that our future will be even greater than before.

All this came upon king Nebuchadnezzar twelve months later. His kingdom was suddenly attacked by the Medes and the Persians. He was driven from men and lived like an animal for seven years. At the end of the days he acknowledged the Most High and his kingdom was restored to him and became even greater than before, because he praised the King of Heaven whose dominion is an everlasting dominion and His kingdom is from generation to generation.

STUMPS ARE STILL ALIVE

I did not realize that a stump can grow back into a huge tree in a relatively short period of time, but I learned this firsthand while traveling through the Sierras in eastern California on business.

Late one night when hauling a truckload of metal, I stopped overnight at a motel in Pine Grove and the next morning during breakfast I met a man at a nearby restaurant. He said the family owns land with redwood trees.

Curious, I asked him how they could chop down a 1200-year-old tree. Wouldn't it take another 1200 years to replace such a tree?"

I was amazed when the man explained to me that because of the massive root system of the 1200-year-old trees, five to seven saplings immediately begin to grow up from the stump.

Within 20 years or so after the huge old tree was cut down the saplings from the stump will be sufficient in size to make harvestable lumber.

This nation will fall just like a huge redwood tree. We will still have a tremendous root structure in place. Following massive widespread destruction and bloodshed of WWIII, our nation will recover, be restored, once again grow and prosper and become even greater than before.

"*Let them be drenched with the dew of heaven; let them live like wild animals till seven times pass by for him.*" This refers to the seven years of tribulation.

I suspect the seven-year period begins with the Nuclear attack on America, that starts World War III. Amid the struggle to survive, Daniel says, people will be driven away to "*...live like wild animals. You'll eat the grass like cattle.*"

This is to continue until "*you acknowledge the most high is solemn over the kingdoms of men.*" When that happens, God's command to leave the tree's stump with its roots intact is so that "*your kingdom will be restored.*"

For this to happen Daniel says we must renounce our sins and do what is right by showing kindness to the oppressed. Otherwise, the soul who sins is the one who will die, such as those killed in the sudden initial nuclear attacks, or the following siege of sickness, contaminated food and water, and people killing each other.

Consider this evidence, in Daniel 11:14 the attacks will occur in the Beautiful Land. And who are we, none other but "America the Beautiful."

Yet, we haven't sought the favor of our Lord by turning from our sins and giving attention to God's word.

"The Lord did not hesitate to bring disaster on us, for the Lord God is righteous in everything he does and we have not obeyed him."

Ezekiel 31 is a similar story about a cedar tree that is just Ezekiel's version of the same tree in Daniel. God has shown the same things to different men at different times. Each man has his own way of describing what he sees by his own words, but the story remains the same. The tree represents the United States of America. And as in the example given to us, both the Medes and the Persians attacked the kingdom of Nebuchadnezzar twelve months later.

WE CAME FROM EGYPT

Ezekiel 20 talks about the Lord bringing the Israelites out of slavery in Egypt and into a land flowing with milk and honey, which is the most beautiful of all lands. We are called "America, The Beautiful." And we are the descendants of those Israelites, who were slaves in Egypt.

The time of the Pharaoh who had the dreams foretelling of the seven years of famine had passed. But when the seven years of famine began, the Pharaoh followed the instructions to store up and prepare for it. When the people began to starve, they came to the Pharaoh and said, "We have nothing to eat, sell us grain lest we die."

And they gave him all of their silver and gold. The second year, the famine persisted, and the people came to the Pharaoh, and said, "We're starving. You have our silver and gold. We have nothing to feed our livestock, and they're starving. Give us grain for ourselves, and we'll give you our livestock."

So, the people survived another year. The famine persisted, and the people came to the Pharaoh and said, "We're starving. You have our silver and gold. You have all of our livestock, and we're in a drought. And our fields yield no crops. Take our land and give us grain lest we die."

The famine persisted. And the people came to the Pharaoh and said, "We're starving. You have our silver and gold, you have all our livestock, and you have all our land, and we have nothing left to give you but ourselves. We will sell ourselves to you as slaves. Give us grain lest we die."

So, you can see that when the seven years of famine ended, and the times returned to normal, the Kingdom of the Pharaoh was extremely wealthy. As far as the dominion of the kingdom extended, it had all the silver and gold, all the herds of livestock, and they multiplied, and the fields once again yielded their crops. And all the people were at the Pharaoh's disposal because they had sold themselves to him.

It stands to reason that the Pharaoh had to find something for all these people to do. It seems like he must have come up with the most massive public works projects in the history of mankind. He began to build the world famous pyramids that still stand today as a lasting monument to his kingdom..

But the time of Joseph and the Pharaoh who had the dream about the seven years of coming the famine had passed. And then arose a new Pharaoh who did not know Joseph. The Egyptians had enslaved all the people of Israel, making their burden heavier, and they were told to get their own straw to make their bricks.

The Israelites were bricklayers. Brickwork is called masonry, and so you can see a connection to the Freemasons of Scotland. Why do they call themselves "free?" Well, it's because they were slaves, but now they're free.

George Washington, who is on our $1 bill, was reported to be a Mason.

There is an Egyptian pyramid on the left side of the reverse of our $1 bill, which I see as the symbol of our beginnings. And the eagle on the right side represents what we have become. The eagle is the United States Government's official emblem. It really does represent our alpha and omega.

The Lord takes pity on his people, and has compassion on them. He prepares Moses to be used by Him to lead the Israelites out of slavery, out of Egypt, and to the Promised Land.

The Lord tells Moses to go to the Pharaoh, and tell him to "let the people go." But the Pharaoh repeatedly hardens his heart, and seven plagues came upon the land of Egypt at that time one of which was gross darkness covering the land for three days and three nights.

It's another example of the Day of the Lord, a day of darkness and gloom. Like a day of nuclear attacks .The Bible says the River Nile began to stink, that all the fish in the river die, and Egyptians couldn't drink the water. This supports what Ezekiel says in Chapter 4, "water will be scarce."

The consistency of God's word confirms the truth of the interpretation. In Isaiah 3, *"take away supplies of water,"* and Jeremiah 8 says, *"The Lord will give them poisoned water to drink."*

The gross darkness covering the land of Egypt is caused by particles floating in the air. It doesn't say if this is smoke, or soot, or ash. But particles in the air eventually come back to earth. That would explain the water in the River Nile becoming a problem.

And it says that the Egyptians had to dig holes along the banks of the River Nile to get water to drink. We can learn a lesson from this example, too.

Radiation fallout from a nuclear explosion will contaminate open bodies of surface water, rivers, ponds and streams. But underground water in domestic wells and municipal wells will remain a clean source of good water to drink—even in a time like this.

I began to see that even the plagues that came upon Egypt also provide a realistic example what it will be like following the Day of the Lord. The United States could experience an interruption of the national power grid. And electricity to run the motors on the pumps in the wells could be a problem for an indefinite period of time. So, a prudent man understanding this would do well to be prepared by having a generator of sufficient capacity to run the motor on the pump in his well.

That generator will be worthless without a quantity of fuel necessary for an extended and indefinite duration.

The Israelites were told to stay inside and close their doors until the plague passed over them. The good news is this plague will also pass over. The Passover is a religious term, but certainly has a practical application in this scenario. In the aftermath of a nuclear attack, it could be essential to survival to stay inside and keep your doors and windows tightly closed until the wind carrying the plague of radiation fallout dust passes over and clean air returns.

I discovered another confirming passage in Isaiah 26 that says, *"Go my people. Enter your rooms and shut the doors behind you; hide yourselves for a little while until his wrath has passed by."* I put this verse into my accumulation of evidence that supports nuclear disaster is coming soon.

In Exodus 9, the Lord even told Moses to take handfuls of soot from a furnace and toss it into the air in the presence of Pharaoh, and it'll become fine dust over the whole land, and festering boils will break out on men and animals alike.

The reason the Lord told Moses to do that is, God wants us to understand what is going to happen. And he has given us example after example for us to learn from.

It even says that in I Corinthians 10. These things—in Israel's history—occurred as examples and warnings for us on whom the end will come. That means all the things that Israel went through in their history happened to them solely for the purpose of providing today's people, knowledge about what's coming upon them in this end-time disaster.

SIMILARITIES TO A NUCLEAR ATTACK

The stories in the Old Testament consistently bare a resemblance or a similarity to the aftermath of a nuclear attack. There are too many similarities to dismiss them as merely coincidences. Can you imagine how much has been done by God to warn us about what will happen at the time of the end? God orchestrated all those events in Israel's history from the foundations of the world for those of us upon whom this climactic end is coming.

After the Egyptians agreed to let the Israelites go, they were led by Moses out of Egypt, then the Pharaoh had a change of heart. With all his army and all his chariots, he set out to get them and bring them back. The Pharaoh's army was closing in on the Israelites, and they were trapped by the Red Sea—with no apparent means of escape.

Right when they thought their doom was imminent—suddenly, by the power of God, the sea parted. And the Lord made a way for them to escape. They crossed over the Red Sea on dry land, but the Pharaoh and his army were right on their heels. No sooner had the Israelites crossed the Red Sea, than the Pharaoh and all his chariots followed right behind them.

Then the waters suddenly came crashing down on the most powerful army in the world at that time. Their pursuers perished at the hand of the Lord. And the Israelites didn't have to so much as lift a finger.

THE ARMIES OF THE BEAST

The Pharaoh's army is a type and shadow of the large and mighty army of 200 million in Revelation 9. They obviously are not assembled of Americans for we are too few, and there simply aren't enough of us. Whoever would go to such great expense and effort to assemble, equip, and mobilize a force of that size must be convinced that there is such a formidable foe that this is the number of them that they will need to be victorious. So we can arrive at no other logical conclusion, but this is a coalition of enemy nations that will be gathered together to destroy us.

The Bible says who can make war against the Beast? The Beast is a war maker and this force of 200 million is who they are. So who do they intend to make war with? It certainly would appear to be the sole remaining super power, the United States and our English speaking allies. It will appear at that time that our doom is imminent. Our weakness—lack of manpower—will be exploited.

THE PATH TO WORLD PEACE

But this time it will be the clouds that part, and the rider on the white horse of Revelations 19 appears, leading the armies of heaven. His eyes are a blazing fire; on his head are many crowns. His name is called Faithful and True, with justice He judges and makes war. On His thigh is written "KING OF KINGS AND LORD OF LORDS."

His robe is dipped in blood. His name is The Word of God. It's the return of Jesus. He's coming to our rescue and to save us from our enemies.

You see there is a path that leads to world peace. Jesus is called "The Prince of Peace" and He is on that path. He has a two-edged sword in his hand, with which to strike down the nations—these wicked godless nations that have formed against us will suddenly be destroyed. The path has a name. It is called "THE WARPATH." Do people at war rallies that chant "no more war" understand that peace comes at a price? I don't think so. They aren't willing to pay the price for peace.

INTERCONTINENTAL BALLISTIC MISSILES

In Revelation 9 John saw a star fall from the sky to the earth. A missile streaks across the sky like a falling star, it leaves a trail of fire in it's wake. The star was given a key and it opened the shaft to the bottomless pit. When a nuclear warhead hits the earth the nuclear energy releases in the form of a shaft and rises up and forms the mushroom cloud.

The shaft is the stem of the mushroom cloud. Up through the shaft rose smoke and fire of a gigantic furnace and the skies became black from the smoke. The internal temperature of the nuclear mushroom cloud is ten million degrees. The agony the men suffer looks like they have been stung by scorpions. What better way for a man of two thousand years ago to describe what radiation sickness looks like?

I am convinced that these missiles have the American flag on them, because after the descriptions of the army of 200 million; the fate that army faces becomes very clear. By the three plagues of fire, smoke, and sulfur, one third of mankind is killed. The Pharaoh's army was destroyed by water, but this time our enemies will be destroyed with fire—thermal nuclear fire.

A third of mankind is over two billion people. How will peace on earth be achieved? It'll be established by the complete and total nuclear destruction of all of our enemies, men, women, and children. There will be no one left to challenge or fight us ever again, because the job will be completely over and done with. Read in Zechariah 14 about what happens to those who fought against us. Their flesh will rot on their bones while they're still standing on their feet; their eyes will rot in their sockets; and their tongues will rot in their mouths. A similar plague will affect all their animals. This is clearly the result of them suffering our nuclear retaliation. There shall be no mercy on them, rightfully so, for they fully intended and attempted to do the same to our entire country. Now, you can see how the new life emerges, that is the result of the seven years of birth pains.

WEEDS GROW UP WITH THE GOOD SEED

How can anyone justify nuclear annihilation of over

two billion people, men women and children—the same way that men, women and children perished in Hiroshima and Nagasaki?

We'll be attacked first, by an unprecedented act of aggression with the devastation of nuclear bombs making what happened in Pearl Harbor seem like child's play.

The Bible tells us in the Parable about the harvest that the master sent the workers out to plant the seed. They returned and said that there were weeds growing up along with the good seed.

When they wanted to go pull up the weeds, they were told it would be better to let them grow up together until the time of the harvest. And then when it's harvest time, first, we'll gather the weeds and burn them.

And then, we'll put the wheat into the barn. A third of mankind will be killed by fire. The logical conclusion is that they must be the bad seed. It is the time of harvest, and the job at hand is to begin gathering the weeds and burning them.

Then, we can put the wheat into the barn, which is the New Age, the Glorious Kingdom of God coming to the earth and it'll be like heaven here. Like the Lord's Prayer says, "Thy kingdom come, thy will be done, here on earth as it is in heaven."

THIS IS THE GLORY OF THE SAINTS

This is the glory of the saints, according to Psalms 149. "*To inflict vengeance on the nations, and punishment on the peoples—to bind their kings with fetters and their nobles with shackles of iron, to carry out the sentence written against them. Praise the Lord.*"

There's also a Passage in Isaiah 2 that says, "*They will beat their swords into plow shares, and their spears into pruning hooks; nation will not take up sword against nation, nor will they train for war anymore.*"

The military budget of the United States is over $400 billion a year. Those resources will be available for something else. The weapons of war are going to become surplus, like World War II surplus. They will be scrapped, no longer needed.

What will be needed are implements of agriculture because the earth is a long ways from achieving its maximum potential of agricultural productivity. In the future, earth-moving equipment will form intercontinental highways. Someday you'll be able to drive non-stop from Cairo to Johannesburg on a freeway, or from Baghdad to Beijing, or from Calcutta to Moscow.

It is interesting to envision the future development of these other continents. They have great potential yet to be maximized.

Mankind will be able to focus on achievements like these, when the threat of war no longer exists.

THE ENORMOUS STATUE

Another biblical story about the time of the end occurs when King Nebuchadnezzar has dreams of an enormous statue, whose head is gold and whose chest is silver, whose belly and thighs are bronze, and legs are iron. The statue's feet are of iron and clay.

I began to understand whom they represent—four kingdoms that rule in succession. The head of gold we are told represents the first kingdom—Nebuchadnezzar.

The chest of silver followed next in time fits the age of the Roman Empire

The last kingdom is the kingdom of iron and clay. It says that in the time of the kings of iron and clay that the god of heaven will come and establish a kingdom on the earth that'll never end.

But that kingdom will crush and bring those kingdoms of iron and clay to an end. I deducted from that, that the kings of iron and clay are ruling at the end of the time of tribulation and are the beast of Revelation 13 who makes war.

I figure the king of clay to be China, because they're the earth's kingdom with the most people—and we're told that people are made out of clay.

RUSSIA IS "PACKING IRON"

I ran into a friend of mine whom I hadn't seen since high school, and when I asked him, "What have you been up to?" he told me he was "packing iron."

I said, "Do you mean you're working for the Iron Worker's Union?"

"No, I'm a security guard at a casino, and I carry a pistol. And we in the security profession refer to carrying a weapon as 'packing iron.'"

Well, I became informed about Russia, which has the world's largest conventional military force. They have three times as many tanks as we do. I thought to myself, they're packing a whole lot of iron. Those tanks weigh something like seventy tons each. That would make Russia the king of iron.

KINGDOM OF BRONZE

And it says that the kingdom of bronze has dominion over the whole earth.

We continue to patrol and control all seven seas of the world since the end of WWII. That is all the international waters and it covers about two-thirds of the earth's surface. I see us a truly having dominion over the whole earth. No nation exists who can challenge us on the high seas.

But, I wondered how is it that we could be referred to as the kingdom of bronze. One day I was digging a trench for a waterline with my backhoe. I had called the 1-800-Dig number, and they had marked all the underground utility lines in the vicinity.

But suddenly, I pulled up with the backhoe bucket a big wad of copper spaghetti. I had ripped through an unmarked 200 pair phone line that had been abandoned. I thought, "Just like when you cut on yourself—a little blood will come out—here in the ground of America. When you scratch it, out comes copper."

And it occurred to me, that the modern world has been encircled with strands of copper. The United States of America has developed and grew along with the growth and development of electricity. With Ben Franklin and a key tied to a kite line, experimenting with lightning—until electricity has transformed life on earth more than any other thing.

Copper is used in generator windings. This yellow metal is the chosen for its electrical conductivity and its abundance.

We have Alexander Graham Bell inventing the telegraph, and Thomas Edison inventing the light bulb followed by the advent of radio, radar, televisions, microwaves, computers, microchips, and other technologies.

Since the beginning of the history of this nation, life has been transformed by electricity. And in addition to having dominion over all the earth, we're the kingdom of bronze.

THE FEET OF THE STATUE SMASHED

This enormous, dazzling statue from the story of King Nebuchadnezzar—awesome in appearance—was struck on its feet of iron and clay by rock cut out, but not by human hands. It got smashed into fine dust, like chaff on a threshing floor in the summer as the wind swept it away without leaving a trace. That's the nuclear devastation of one third of the earth's population, per Revelations 9:18.

Who are they, but the tares that are going to be gathered and burned at the time of the harvest? It is the end that comes upon our enemies—the kings of iron and clay, of Daniel 2:44.

At that same time the God of heaven sets up His kingdom that will never end and it begins to fill the whole earth with a never- ending expansion.

But the rock, not made by human hands, that struck the statue, became a huge mountain, and filled the whole earth. That is the Coming Kingdom of Heaven on the Earth That Will Never Be Destroyed. Thy kingdom come, thy will be done here on earth as it is in heaven.

THE KINGDOM OF HEAVEN COMES TO EARTH

What if you could go back in time a hundred years ago and sit around a campfire talking to the men of that time period. You could ask them what do you suppose life on earth will be like in another hundred years. None of them even with the wildest imaginations could ever come close to describing this modern day and all that exists. In the same way life on earth in another hundred years will be so advanced we cannot comprehend the way it is going to be. War will be a thing of the past. The vast amount of resources spent on military budgets will be available for other things like research. Now take the next hundred years and try to see where this planet will be for ten more one hundred year periods of time. The future truly surpasses all of your wildest dreams.

CHAPTER 13

THE FIRST OF THE FOUR BEASTS HAS RISEN

Another end-time story is in Daniel's chapter 7 about four beasts. They rise up out of the sea at the time of the end. The first one is a lion with wings of an eagle.

The lion represents the United Kingdom as the official emblem; the eagle represents the United State of America. Its wings were torn off, and it stood on two feet, and the heart of a man was given to it. This same time period and events are also described in other scriptures: *"The people will get a new heart..."* Ezekiel 18:31.

In the same way that the ram in Daniel 8 gets its horn broken off, but the goat isn't killed, the tree in Daniel 4 gets cut down but the life in the stump remains, Jeremiah repeatedly says in Chapter 5, *"Do not destroy them completely."*

Hope of recovery remains, and even an eagle's feathers can grow back—so can new saplings grow from a stump that still has life and a goat with it's horn broken off is still alive. In each of these cases there is not complete destruction.

The first beast has risen, and it is the War on Terrorism, the attack of Yugoslavia, the attacking of Iraq, and George Bush and Tony Blair walking across the White House lawn, waging war together, both in complete agreement.

I saw a documentary about our aircraft carriers. It takes ten years from the beginning of constructing one till its completion. In this initial attack on America, if our enemies can successfully sink our aircraft carriers—our air superiority would be lost. Air superiority is essential in today's military conflicts to achieve victory. That could be the eagle's wing feathers being torn off because the second beast is called the bear, which is told to "go devour much flesh."

THE SECOND BEAST

The bear has three ribs in its mouth. The devouring of much flesh is The Day of the Lord. Russia is referred to as a bear. Russia is coming from out of the north. That nation also is the king of iron. And Jeremiah 15:12 says, *"Can a man break iron from the north, or bronze?"*

There are the bands of iron and bronze on the tree stump. But when Massachusetts Senator John Kerry was campaigning against President Bush in 2004—and being critical of the military action in Iraq—he referred to President Bush's 30-nation coalition force as being coerced and bribed.

Kerry said that there were only three nations who initiated the attack on Iraq." Those three nations, I thought, might be who the three ribs are in the bear's mouth. That's the United States, the United Kingdom, and Australia. The United Nations Secretary General has declared the United States' attack as illegal and in violation of international law. So International Law has been broken by the Bush administration. You may have heard it said "THE LAW IS THE LAW—NO ONE IS ABOVE THE LAW."

I suspect the enemies of the United States are demanding that we be brought to justice. Who else can the United Nations turn to, in order to enforce international law against the United States, other than the Russian bear? With Russia's weaken economy one might not think that they pose much of a threat, but they have tripled their military budget since Putin assumed leadership. Also their long-standing nuclear arms policy that only authorized use in the event of an attack against Russia has been reversed to now allow them to initiate a pre-emptive strike if they perceive a threat exists. We clearly have provided them with that existing threat. Acting under the authority of the United Nations they would receive compensation for enforcing international law and at the same time turn the financial burden of their military into a profit.

I don't see Russian leader Putin as the kind of man who is told what to do, but he could become the United Nation's hired gun. For the Bible tells us that the bear is told to "go, devour much flesh."

COMPARING THE PAST TO THE PRESENT

As in the case of Desert Storm in the early 1990s, the United Nations authorized the United States to attack Saddam and end his aggression on Kuwait. The United Nations was formed in part for the purpose of maintaining world peace, and if any country becomes an aggressor nation by attacking others—like Hitler did in the beginning of World War II—it will be stopped. In other words, nipping it in the bud before things get out of hand.

However, today's United Nations doesn't possess this international law enforcement capability. So, when they see a direct violation of International Law, such as Saddam invading Kuwait—or President Bush openly and defiantly telling them that he is going to attack Iraq and remove Saddam from power, with or without their permission—they become enraged.

Their authority has been challenged. The very justification for their existence is questionable if the are impotent or have no teeth. There are members of the United Nations Security Council who cannot particularly be counted as allies of America. These enemy voices are ceaselessly demanding that the United States must be brought to justice.

Russia has a tremendous amount of military resources and they have the largest conventional army in the world. And just like a hired gun looking for a job, they could use the money. In the same way that the United Nations compensated the United States Military for its Desert Storm action of enforcing the international law against Saddam, so compensation could be offered to Russia to enforce international law against the United States.

THE THIRD BEAST

The third beast is a four-headed leopard, given authority to rule. This story parallels the tale of the ram and the goat because the goat has its prominent horn broken off before four other horns grow in its place. Through the process of elimination of major world powers, the leopard is likely made up of holy jihadist Christian hating Muslim nations like Iran, Iraq, Libya, Syria, who were included on the list of the seven nations in the Pentagon's prepared plans for nuclear war along with Russia, China, and North Korea.

BEWARE OF THE FOURTH BEAST

The fourth beast is more dreadful and terrifying than all the others. And it has large teeth of iron, and it'll be different from all the other kingdoms. And it'll devour the whole earth—trampling it down and crushing it.

It has ten horns—which are ten kings who come from this kingdom. And the saints will be handed over to them for a time, times and half a time—which some consider to be three and one-half years.

I think this marks the last half of the seven years of tribulation. This scripture talks about none other than today's China, which now possesses the world's second largest navy, surpassed only by the United States for the time being. After the invading Russian coalition falls on the mountains of the Israel of Ezekiel 39 (USA), China will take notice that the two major world powers that dominated post WWII era are now militarily and economically seriously weakened. They will begin to make their move for world domination—crushing and devouring the whole earth.

For the past twenty-some years Chinese couples have only been allowed to have one baby. In Chinese culture the boy is considered more desirable than a girl. With most couples choosing to have baby boys, the news recently reported their young male population is now estimated at one hundred and thirty million. They will make up the main part of Revelation 9's 200 million mounted troops.

With an army of 200 million, they will begin to tromp-tromp-tromp across that face of the earth crushing and devouring one nation after another. Confident that nothing can stop us now, will be their attitude. China ridicules our Christian faith. They think we are like kindergartners who still believe in Santa Clause. They are convinced that the notion that Jesus rose from the dead and will ever come again is purely a fairy tale. It will be the greatest miscalculation in all of military warfare.

They are the third of mankind who are killed by fire, smoke and sulfur. They are the clay feet of the dazzling statue that is smashed and turns into fine dust that blows away. They are the tares that are gathered into bundles to be burned.

EDEN VALLEY

As I was driving through California, on a trip to pick up a military surplus diesel generator, the words of Chapter 2 of the Book of Joel echo in my mind. It says: "A large and mighty army comes, such as never was of old, nor ever will be in ages to come, before them the fire burns and behind them the flames blaze; before them the land lies like the garden of Eden, behind them a desolate waste."—The Day of the Lord.

Observation of the immaculately manicured vineyards and orchards spreading out as far as I could see in every direction convinced me that this place fits the description like the Garden of Eden. Right with those thoughts running through my mind, I drove right past a green road sign with big white capitol letters on it that read "EDEN VALLEY."

When I tell you the Lord has shown me many signs, this is literally one of them. Again God confirms to me that the scriptures do apply to this great land, and it is us who will be invaded.

Joel does go on to say that the Lord will drive that northern army back out across a parched and barren land. That is the land they burned as they invaded, so you can see that they will be turned around the same as it says in Ezekiel 38 & 39. They come from out of the far north, a great horde, fully armed, with Persia among them. But the bow will be struck from their left hand, and the arrows will drop from their right hand. And they will fall. The Lord will deliver us from all those enemies at that time. How do you suppose the Lord accomplishes His purposes? He uses human vessels. His servants carry out His will. We have a war to fight and we better get ready now. There is not enough of us, so we had better be as prepared as possible.

God wants you to know of these warnings, and to survive. And he wants you to read every word of this document. Just like I do, God loves you, and he wants the best for you.

Even among those who hear of my warnings, the notion of a nuclear attack is overwhelming. There's a similar mentality across America; most people refuse to think about it. There is a verse that says "what they fear the most will come upon them".

What is feared more than a nuclear holocaust?

I recall the 1970s when county governments had trucks embossed with civil defense emblems. Partly through support from the federal government, officials mandated or encouraged bomb shelters and civil defense programs. Some buildings offered protection against bombs, and various former mine facilities were designated as civil defense shelters.

Yet in the wake of such programs being stopped or curtailed, many people today decline to even discuss the danger. They're making a big mistake. This beast is now rising. America's enemies are forming a military alliance into what the Bible refers to as "the beast." Revelations 13 asks this: Who can make war against the beast? What is the beast? It is very simple. The beast is a war maker. Who else could they be making war with but the sole remaining super power—the United States of America?

WHO IS THE BEAST IN REVELATION 17?

Seven nations will form a military alliance referred to as the Beast. Revelations 17 says the beast has seven heads—five of which have fallen, while "one is, and the other is yet to come."

While visiting China in late 1999, Yeltsin told the Chinese leader that, "It seems President Clinton has forgotten that Russia still is a world power who possesses a nuclear arsenal." With the emphasis on **is**.

Russia remained undefeated after World War II. I've concluded that indeed, the head that **"is"** represents Russia—while the head that "is to come" represents China with its military build up and emerging, mushrooming, snowballing economy, and industrial power.

The five heads that have fallen include Germany and France, which both fell in World War II and have opposed the United States' attack on Iraq. Japan also fell hard and I have been told by some that the Japanese are never going to forget it or get over it. I am not sure who all five of the fallen heads are; as time passes I am sure it will become clear.

Further evidence making this threat a reality, Russia and Germany have recently strengthened their alliances with China. These nations share many common views on major international issues while forming an alliance that polarizes against the United States.

In fact, when forming and solidifying this alliance in 2004, Germany and China proclaimed they share a desire to make important contributions in establishing worldwide peace and stability. Germany's chancellor Schroeder openly stated this when arriving at the Beijing airport.

But who do Germany and China think is disturbing the peace or causing instability? From their point of view, it's the United States. These countries are forming a strategic partnership. Their common bond is their growing contempt for American domination.

Revelations 13 also warns that the beast has the feet of a bear, and it gets its power from the dragon. The general consensus is that the bear represents Russia.

That nation has the world's largest conventional forces and three times as many tanks as the United States. Today, military leaders depend on tanks for ground movement, like feet that are used to walk on the ground. The Russian tanks are the feet of the bear. At fifty tons each their tanks represent a great deal of iron. They are who it is in Daniel 2, the "King of Iron", and as in Jeremiah 15:12, "who can break iron from the north?" The Russian Federation from the north is those of Jeremiah chapter 1 and Ezekiel chapter 38 and 39. Persia is with them.

On the news one day, U.S. Secretary of Defense Donald Rumsfeld stated that the Bush administration was making the missile defense system a top priority. But he made it clear that it wasn't because of Russia and their nuclear arsenal. He no longer considered Russia as much of a threat as it once had been because of their weakened economy.

It stands to reason that the threat of an attack or making war requires considerable financial resources, without which not much can be accomplished.

Nations are forming and strengthening their alliances because together they can pool their resources—equipment, manpower, finances—to become an imposing, unified military power, capable of challenging the United States for world domination.

I saw a Chinese New Year's parade on the news, in which a huge dragon made its way down the main street at Tiananmen Square. We're told the beast gets its power from the dragon, and so the dragon represents China who has lots of money—giving it the power to finance war.

"FAR RICHER THAN THE OTHERS"

Daniel Chapter 11 warns that, "...three more kings will appear in Persia, and then a fourth who will be far richer than the others, When he has gained power by his wealth, he'll stir up everyone against the kingdom of Greece, and then a mighty king will appear who will rule with great power and do as he pleases." Who can this be?

Today, the ancient Bible lands of Persia span the Middle East region. China is becoming far richer than the others. In 2005 China's world trade surplus exceeded 1.4 trillion dollars.

Like it was before WWII, now in today's world the two polarizing forces can be referred to as the free world and the slave world. But in Daniel 11, it's the kingdom of Persia and the kingdom of Greece.

Senators lead the United States government—just like the senators of ancient Athens, Greece. I see these references to Greece as they equate to modern Washington, D.C. where numerous government buildings are in the ancient Greek architectural style—embossed with words such as "Aristotle."

Imagine if you took Daniel or Ezekiel of Biblical fame on a helicopter tour of our nation's capitol today with all of the Greek architecture, they could easily assume our nation's capitol to be the modern capitol Greek city of Athens as it has evolved many years into the future.

Our enemies are certainly becoming stirred up, aren't they?

President George W. Bush seems like the mighty king who rules with great power and does as he pleases. Retired U.S. Secretary of State Lawrence Eagleburger, a seasoned expert in international affairs, stated during a TV interview that the day is coming when it will become impossible for the United States to maintain military superiority over China.

This mighty king's empire is to be broken up and uprooted and given to others. Could it be this United States?

666 THE MARK OF THE BEAST

I had read about the time of Nero Caesar that it was believed he was the anti-christ because the letters of his name when translated into Hebrew added up to 666 because every Hebrew letter has a numerical equivalent. With this information I found that the letter w = 6. I had heard that computers would be used to control all the buying and selling and without an account to access you will not be able to buy or sell. So it is simple 666 =WWW. World wide web. It is not hard to see how things can come to this in the future. To participate in the future global economy you will be assigned a number or mark. You must not engage in this diabolical system. Barter or trade for labor will be your only means of continuing to survive until the Lord returns.

THE ANTICHRIST IS RISING UP

If the Holy Spirit began to move across the land, it would be called a revival. You would see people loving and forgiving one another. But today there is a movement of the spirit of the antichrist and it is evidenced by the mentality of hatred toward Americans and Christians everywhere.

A recent issue of the "Voice of the Martyrs" a Christian magazine gave compelling details of how countries worldwide are persecuting Christians. Remember, the vast majority of Americans hail from Christianity—the cornerstone in the founding of our country.

In a copyrighted article, the magazine listed in detail that:

1 MUSLIMS: People of this faith are persecuting and harassing Christians in those nations.

2 WORLDWIDE: Governments or people from various religions in forty-two countries seek to harm Christians and stop Christianity.

3 GOVERNMENTS: Some governments now structure their societies in a manner that encourages violence against those who follow the word of Christ.

4 DIVERSITY: Although some nations other than the United States boast diverse societies of many people and religions, in other countries there's often little tolerance like ours. The magazine says that in India, for instance, "...radical Hindus have become increasingly open in their conflict with Christians."

CHAPTER 14

U.S. GOVERNMENT CONTINUES ITS WARNINGS

New Year's Day approached at the end of 2003, for a brief period top U.S. officials raised the terror alert to the high orange level. Authorities explained that government intelligence had reported a high incidence of chatter on the Internet by terrorists about an attack on multiple cities that will "Make 911 pale by comparison." I instantly figured that it is the "Day of the Lord" they are planning. Our government continued to make every effort to protect us. They had helicopters continuously circling several major cities, but no attack has taken place yet. But you can bet that it is still in the making, because of the determination of these enemies, they are not going to go away.

Because more terrorist attacks are anticipated by our government, it has a toll free, 24-hour number for citizens to get advice just dial: *"1-800-BE-READY."*

They will ask for a name and address to sent you a packet of instructions for free

Keep in mind that specific situations and spur-of-the-moment survival strategies will vary, depending on your location and the wind direction. Even so, as in the time-tested Boy Scout motto, in all cases at least one constant remains, "Be Prepared."

We must prepare to take every reasonable precaution. Among them:

1 GASOLINE: The U.S. Government Department of Homeland Defense recommends all motorists ensure that their

gas tanks are kept as full as possible at all times. We are being told to go and fill up at the gas station even when your tank is still half full. You don't want to be caught almost out of gas when a sudden disaster occurs. You may not have time to go get gas in order to flee. Keep some additional gas jugs or even a tank on a stand on your own property if you can. We have become helpless without fuel. Take a lesson from our government—they have what is called the national strategic fuel reserves. That is fuel for them, not for you. You can and should have your own private strategic fuel reserve. Any prudent man can understand how foolish it is to assume that whenever he wants fuel he can always just go down to the gas station and fill up. A nuclear attack will stop all distribution of supplies including fuel, and the highways will be deserted. Is that because there is no fuel? That is exactly what Isaiah 3:1-2 and Isaiah 33 says.

2 GEIGER COUNTERS: Without one of these you could enter into a death zone and not even know it. You can acquire inexpensive World War II surplus Geiger counters. They can be found on-line by search engines. Survivors will need to be able to detect and designate safe areas as well as danger zones.

3 CLOTHING: War will bring the imported clothing industry to a screeching halt. Your existing clothes will have to last you for some time. Have extra clothing on hand, suitable to keep you comfortable year-round. Be prepared for all types of weather, from extreme cold to exhausting heat.

4 POWER GENERATORS: Purchase and maintain efficient power generators capable of lasting long periods. Fuel supplies are going to be scarce so stock up now. You may need to survive off the primary power grid for at least a year or longer.

5 DIESEL FUEL: Stock up on diesel fuel, gasoline and propane. I prefer vehicles and generators that use diesel, because it has a longer shelf life than gasoline and may be more plentiful. Propane can also be stored indefinitely.

6 BATTERIES: Have enough batteries for all equipment requiring it, stockpiles sufficient for a one-year period. This way you'll avoid having flashlights with nothing to power them. And

remember, portable radios might be able to pick up any station that manages to get on the air with stand-by power.

7 SEAL WINDOWS: Be sure to seal windows tight now rather than face severe illness or potential death from radiation. Your chances of survival and continued good health increase by avoiding inhaling or ingesting even fine dust contaminated with radiation. I have acquired some clean air purifiers to remove any radiation dust from inside the house.

Be encouraged for this coming punishment is coming upon the wicked, Isaiah 3:10 says to tell the righteous that it will be well with them; for they will enjoy the fruit of their deeds. But the noble man makes noble plans and by noble deeds he will stand. (Isaiah 32:8) Yet you can survive by planning for the attack.

THE BIBLE WARNS OF RADIATION SICKNESS

The Bible clearly warns that those who fail to heed these warnings face severe or deadly radiation sickness. In Deuteronomy 28:24, we learn that the consequences of their disobedience will turn the rain of the land into dust and powder coming down from the sky until you are destroyed.

In the preceding verses we're told that the Lord will strike them with a "wasting disease, fever, inflammation, scorching" along with heat, blight, drought, and tumors from which victims cannot be cured. Such symptoms will include scabs, sores, and itching from which they cannot be cured. This is only part of the consequences of their disobedience.

We know from science and previous nuclear disasters that people suffering excessive radiation exposure suffer nausea, lose weight, and can't hold down food. The inability to absorb nutrition lowers the body's resistance to infection. A personal supply of antibiotics may save your life in this coming time when the availability may be scarce.

THE PEOPLE PERISH FOR LACK OF KNOWLEDGE

People today need to know the complexity of radiation exposure. Numerous scientific articles, including one posted on the Internet, note that most people don't know how fast fallout decays. This decrease in intensity/danger happens in a relatively short period. For instance, in a thirty-mile by thirty-mile area directly downwind from a missile field that gets dozens of hits, 100% of people die within six minutes of exposure in areas reaching 10,000 rads per hour.

The level of rads in that same area decreases to 1,000 in that same zone within seven hours. Still 100 percent of people die within just one hour of exposure at that level.

After two days, that drops to 100 rads per hour, and fifty percent of people die within three or four hours of continuous exposure. Finally, in fourteen weeks that decreases to one rad per hour—where fifty percent of people will still die after one month of continuous exposure, and five percent die within fifteen days.

Also, the danger would be far less downwind in a ninety-from a single one-megaton ground burst. Radiation doesn't show up in those areas till seven hours after the blast, arriving at a rate of just fifty rads per hour—when fifty percent of people die after eighteen hours of continuous exposure.

This decreases to just 0.05 rads of exposure in fourteen weeks, when people can stay in those zones without serious health problems.

Knowing this, survivors should strive to keep exposure to minimal periods of time. For instance, if you're downstairs hiding in a basement, beginning fourteen weeks after the attack, you could go upstairs to briefly retrieve things.

Everything depends on how far you are from the blast zone, coupled with the speed and direction and of wind currents, and the amount of radiation emitted per hour in that region. I wholeheartedly recommend the following instructions from God's word.

"Seek the Lord, and seek righteousness and humility; perhaps you will be sheltered on the day of the Lord's anger. Zephaniah 2:3

CHAPTER 15

TIMING REVEALED—THE WEEK—THE MONTH—THE YEAR

Right after the Bush administration publically announced that they were all through playing cat and mouse games with Saddam. The inspectors were not able to find any weapons of mass destruction. But they said he had violated UN resolution 1441 and committed material breaches so they told everyone that he is all through. They are going to take him out. The attack on Iraq was pending. At that time on the news two retired United States generals were being interviewed. They were asked when they thought the attack would take place. The response of the highly trained expert further confirmed what I already knew. He said "the best time for an attack is at night". Attacking amid darkness can leave an enemy confused and inefficient, emphasizing and utilizing the element of surprise. The darker it is the better, because with the sophisticated technology of night vision equipment we have the advantage.

He then stated that the darkest nights are during the new moon!

Once again, I knew the Lord was confirming to me what I already believed. This coming nuclear attack will be in one of the darkest nights during the phase of the new moon.

In addition, Matthew 24:20 tells us to pray that your flight will not occur during the winter, or on the Sabbath.

If the attack hits in summer but not during winter, where is it likely to occur? Is the whole world a target, or is a specific area endangered? Summer is seasonal to only one half of the earth at a time because the other half is experiencing winter..

Similar advice is repeated throughout the Bible. In Luke 22:36, the Lord said, if you have a purse, take it; and if you don't have a sword, sell your coat and buy one. It will be important to have the ability to defend yourself and your loved ones in a time of such turmoil. Exercise your constitutional rights to bear arms. But why are you told to go ahead and sell your coat to buy one?

Coats will not be necessary, as this sudden disaster will occur at the time of the year when summer is near or just beginning. This is the time when even the nights are hot, so you won't be needing a coat.. There will be opportunities to acquire another coat before the cold of winter comes.

390 YEARS OF TOBACCO SMOKING

The Bible clearly supports this link to tobacco in Ezekiel Chapter 8. In discussing the wicked things that they are doing, it mentions that seventy elders from the house of Israel each holding a censor in their hand; as a cloud of incense rises in the room. This house of Israel has 390 years of sin for which it is going to suffer 390 days of punishment.

A cloud of incense rising in a room is simply a cloud of smoke in the air. Just like in a room where smokers congregate together.

Ezekiel says each one of them was holding censors in their hands. A "censor" is a fire resistant container that contains a smoldering substance from which smoke rises. He is describing in the words of his time- the best as he can- a group of men smoking tobacco pipes. A pipe was the original method of smoking in the early 1600s, before the introduction of cigars and cigarettes.

Then I read in my local newspaper a full-page ad— "TOBACCO KILLS"—describing the dangers of tobacco. The ad says more than twice as many people die yearly from tobacco than from heroin, cocaine, crack, AIDS, alcohol, murder, suicide, and car accidents combined.

Sponsored by organizations including the American Cancer Society and the American Heart Association, the American Lung Association their message puts the evil of tobacco into perspective.

Today, tobacco use kills millions of people yearly, while driving overall medical costs to staggering levels. The pain and suffering have reached staggering, mind-boggling levels too great to reverse despite multi-billion dollar tobacco industry settlements.

Lobbyists from this economic segment and other major concerns play a key role in influencing Congress, in a system where money rules.

SMOKING TOBACCO IS EVIL

Tobacco is the deadliest killer in the history of the world. No nation, race, or color is exempt from its ravages today..

The highly addictive nicotine in tobacco becomes increasingly difficult for smokers to stop; some smokers swear it's impossible to kick the habit. Once you are addicted, you smoke until you die before your time from lung cancer or suffocating lung failure like emphysema. Some addicted smokers even have to carry around an oxygen tank while still continuing to smoke. Smokers eventually find themselves out of breath, with no strength and can get no relief from their self-afflicted predicament.

The scriptures proclaim, *"Whatever you yield yourself to, that you will become enslaved by."* This holds true for cigarettes which studies show can become more difficult to stop using than heroin.

The first English colony of Jamestown was desperately struggling and called a wretched failure. But in the exact words of one history book "tobacco saved the colony." It became the economic basis of Jamestown and this country's beginning.

Because of the enormous price tobacco sold for, the farmers planted tobacco on every available place on their properties and even in the streets. All they wanted to grow was tobacco.

The problem of farmers growing only tobacco became so

severe that the first legislation that had to be passed required each of them to dedicate a portion of their land to grow food.

OUR NATION WAS FOUNDED ON TOBACCO BUSINESS

England is included as a target of this coming nuclear attack. It is the English who started the commercialization of tobacco on a full-scale basis and delivered the first commercial shipment of Virginian grown tobacco to London in late June 1616. And that was 390 years ago. While establishing the colonies, England promoted tobacco into the fabric of European society. According to various sources of history which I have become increasingly skeptical of the reliability, they have now accumulated the 390 years of sin for which they will now bear the 390 days of siege/punishment. They fit the description of those among the house of Israel.

In addition to worshipping an idol of jealousy, the sin of the house of Israel is described in Ezekiel 8 where Ezekiel is told to go see the wicked things they are doing. So he went and looked, and he saw 70 elders in a room with a cloud of incense rising; and each held a censor in their hand. The cloud of incense rising is a cloud of smoke in the room. Every man is holding in his hand a censor. As mentioned earlier this censor is a small container that is fire retardant which holds a smoldering substance from which smoke rises. Doesn't that sound exactly the same as a tobacco pipe?

It's the English mainly who are guilty of introducing and spreading the use of tobacco to the human race and economically profiting by promoting it, although at that time they were ignorant of the devastating consequences.

THE GROWTH OF TOBACCO

1 1612: A small test plot of tobacco was planted by John Rolfe, and he successfully learned how to grow and cure tobacco in the colonies.

2 1613: Success from the previous test year motivated him

to plant a sizable crop. Late in this year, that crop was harvested and put into caves to dry and be cured.

3 1614: This crop was loaded onto ships in the spring, and it arrived in London in June. Mister Rolfe could not have anticipated the outrageous demand that it was met by. As a result, at least one historian refers to the sale of tobacco in London as the most momentous event of the entire 17th Century, equal to the 1849 gold rush of California. The discovery of how lucrative the sale of tobacco was inspired John Rolfe to return and grow as much as he could possibly get planted the next year.

4 1615: This year is the beginning of the commercialization of growing tobacco for sale. This commercial-size crop was harvested at the end of the year and placed in caves to dry and cure for shipment in the spring of 1616.

5 1616: That year, exactly 390 years before 2006, tobacco became a full-scale commercial enterprise in the colonies.

Understanding Isaiah 29:1 Add year to year is instructions pertaining to the timing of this event of sudden destruction as well as Ezekiel 4:4 the days of siege are the same as the years of their sin. It is a simple mathematical formula forecasting the year of the disaster that is coming. The problem is how to know what year the Lord begins to count their sins from. God's Holy Word is 100% reliable but historians are human and who today knows for sure what exactly is happening 390 years ago?

ONE MORE YEAR?

The solid case can be made for 2006 to be the year of the Day of the Lord, when the birth pains that produce new age shall begin, but we are now passed. So, still the time to prepare is now, not later. Now, December 27, 2007, I am positive we will see the fulfillment of all these things before another summer passes.

The following stories provide for an additional twelve month extension of time.

It was twelve months later that King Nebuchadnezzar's kingdom was cut down. [DANIEL 4:28].

ALSO IN LUKE 13:6 IS A TREE THAT ISN'T BEARING FRUIT, SO THE OWNER WANTS TO CUT IT DOWN,

BUT THE CASE IS MADE TO SPARE IT FOR JUST ONE MORE YEAR AND IT WILL BE DUG AROUND AND FERTILIZED WITH HOPE THAT IT MIGHT PRODUCE FRUIT, BUT IF NOT THEN IT WILL BE CUT DOWN. SO FIGURE THERE MAY BE ANOTHER YEAR TO GO.

THAT WOULD INDICATE THERE MAY BE ANOTHER BEFORE YEAR THE UNITED STATES WILL FALL LIKE A HUGE AND ENORMOUS TREE.

It is American society that fits the description of the sins of the house of Judah, for they turned their backs on the Lord, filled their land with violence, and provoked the Lord to anger by putting the twig to their nose.

These scriptures are describing the last forty years of American society, with the hippy movement—the drugs snorting up the nose to which law enforcement statistics have linked 90% of the violent crime in the land to. But God is very provoked by the Supreme Court ruling that prayer could no longer be allowed in the public schools of America. That is turning our backs on the Lord. It is especially offensive to Him because the heritage of the Lord is godly children, and we are told to teach our children in the ways of the Lord. But in the whole country all the children are sent to the public schools where we won't let them pray, and the Bible is not allowed to be publicly read.

Another supporting fact is that Judah was the son of Israel and in comparison The United States is the son of England. The English introduced tobacco 390 years ago and this country turned it's back on the Lord 40 years ago. Two separate numbers both go back in time to separate and different events that fit what is described as occurring in those past frames. Isn't that a little too freaky to ignore?

EZEKIEL PROVIDES A FORMULA FORETELLING THE YEAR

EZ 4:5 - THE SAME NUMBER OF DAYS AS THE YEARS OF THEIR SIN.

EZ 4:6 - A DAY FOR EACH YEAR

EZ 8:9-11 SEE THE WICKED THINGS THEY ARE DOING, THEY'RE HOLDING CENSORS IN THEIR HANDS & A CLOUD OF INCENCE IS RISING

THE YEAR SIN BEGINS

THE YEAR OF THE LORD

390 YEARS OF SMOKING TOBACCO

390 YEARS OF SIN

SUDDEN DESTRUCTION

CAUSE OF DEATHS

1609 - 600 ENGLISHMEN
1610 - COME TO NEW WORLD
1611 - COLONY OF JAMESTOWN DESPERATELY STRUGGLING
1612 - LEARNED HOW TO GROW & CURE TOBACCO
1613 - THE FIRST CROP GROWN TO BE SOLD IN LONDON
1614 - FIRST SALE OF TOBACCO IN LONDON
1615 - FIRSTCOMMERCIAL CROP PLANTED - TOBACCO TRANSFORMS COLONY INTO RAGING BOOM TOWN
1616 - FIRST COMMERCIAL SHIPMENT OF TABACCO SOLD IN LONDON
1617 - ONE YEAR LATER - CUT DOWN THE TREE <USA> LUKE 13:6-9
      DANIEL 4:29

TOBACCO

AUTOS
SUICIDE
MURDER
ALCOHOL
AIDS
CRACK
COCAINE
HEROIN

TOBACCO KILLS TWICE AS MANY PEOPLE AS HEROIN, COCAIN, CRACK, AIDS, ALCOHOL, MURDER, SUICIDE AND AUTOMOBILE EVERY YEAR!

ISAIAH 29:1 ADD YEAR TO YEAR -

MY LEG BROKE A SECOND TIME

I set out with determination to trust in the Lord to heal my leg. The scriptures say the Lord is our healer, our provider, and our protector.

So, I continued to go to work and used a cane sometimes while limping and gimping along on my half-healed leg. The pain persisted continuously as I walked on what the doctors called a non-union tibia, the shinbone. My weight was being supported by the fibula, the smaller of the two bones in the lower leg

While I conducted a work estimate at a remote Virginia City Highlands home, my good leg slipped on the loose gravel. All my weight suddenly shifted to the weak and sore half-healed leg. I heard a loud snap as the fibula broke and I fell to the ground under the twisting strain of my full weight. The intense pain almost made me pass out but I only saw stars for a while. As I laid there in the backyard in agonizing pain the sky became dark with storm clouds blocking out what had been a sunny day. A very cold wind began to blow spitting snow flakes around me. It occurred to me that because no one was home and I did not even know if or when they would be coming home that I had to get myself back to my truck. I began to very slowly crawl across the sharp rocky ground dragging my broken leg behind. I finally reached my truck after about an hour and drove myself about thirty miles to the hospital in Carson City. Although I tried to take it slow and easy every bump in the road jammed the exposed nerves in the sharp fragmented bones together. I did make it to the hospital and they put my broken leg in a cast.

The tibia—commonly known as the shin bone—remained broken and had failed to heal properly for three and one-half years—just like the halfway point in what I call the seven years of tribulation that culminates with end-time.

While recovering from the second break, I thought about the scripture in Ezekiel 4 that says after you finish 390 days on your left side, to "lie down a second time" for forty more days. Amazingly, that's the exact amount of time for my leg to heal completely. Without consulting any doctors about it, I decided to get up at the end of six weeks of staying home. And without putting a lot of weight on my leg, and I began to try and walk on it. It felt fairly solid so I started to go ahead and increase the weight on it and I have been using it ever since. You see, the amazing thing is that both the bones in my lower leg were now grown together, and they were healed. I returned to work. It had been forty-two days of time I had been laid up. And now my leg is fully healed. As I previously mentioned that both the Pharaoh who dreamt the two dreams and laid down two times and Ezekiel laid down a second time, so did I.

I never hoped for or planned for these events to happen, but when they occurred on their own, I observed the parallel to all these key scriptures vital to timing the end of this age.

ALL THESE INDICTMENTS ARE LISTED IN THE SCRIPTURES

Simply stated, it's why the Lord is going to permit our enemies to attack us. It's our punishment for everything from tobacco use and drugs to promiscuity, immorality to perversion and turning our backs on God, idol worship, materialism and much more.

Isaiah Chapter 1 states that

4 Ah, sinful nation,
    a people loaded with guilt,
    a brood of evildoers,
    children given to corruption!
    They have forsaken the LORD;
    they have spurned the Holy One of Israel
    and turned their backs on him.

5 Why should you be beaten anymore?
    Why do you persist in rebellion?
    Your whole head is injured,
    Your whole heart afflicted.

6 From the sole of your foot to the top of your head
   There is no soundness—
   Only wounds and welts
   And open sores,
   Not cleansed or bandaged
   Or soothed with oil.

Open sores include the site of the former World Trade
Center attacked Sept. 11, 2001. Large areas of devastation from
the hurricanes Katrina and Rita still remain vastly un-restored.
Wildfires that burned ten thousand cattle to death parched
thousands of acres. The worst tornado season on record has
taken I don't know how many lives, and destroyed millions of
dollars of real estate. Therefore:

7 Your country is desolate,
   your cities burned with fire;
   your fields are being stripped by foreigners
   right before you,
   laid waste as when overthrown by strangers.
   Nevertheless, several times within Isaiah and Jeremiah, the
Lord says that we will not be destroyed completely—leaving us
with a hope for the future.

CHAPTER 16

THE GREATEST GENERATION

On April 29, 2004, at the Russell Senate Office Building in Washington, D.C., I attended The Legacy of Heroes reception marking the dedication of the World War II Memorial.

Republican U.S. Sen. John Warner of Virginia spoke at the reception and said that the World War II soldiers were the "greatest generation."

Afterward I spoke with the Senator and told him I had a T-shirt featuring an image of a World War II fighter pilot. Below it said, "The Greatest Generation." At first I liked it; my friends complemented me on it, but the more I thought about, I began to question it.

War is not a thing of the past; it is still looming in our future.

I told the Senator, "I have to respectfully disagree with you; they may have been the greatest generation up to that time. But they didn't finish the job. Now the burden is on this generation today, and now is the time to finish the job. And that is the impending destiny of today's generation. They are the greatest generation because they are going to get the job finished."

The words of Isaiah 2 will come true—never again will nation rise up against nation, and never again will men train for war. The swords will be beat into plowshares, and the spears into pruning hooks.

In order to lead our nation, these officials need to know the importance of our challenge. The great senator said I was right.

Later that same week I returned home from my Washington, D.C. trip, I saw U.S. Secretary of Defense Donald Rumsfeld on the TV news, telling troops in Iraq that those who battled in World War II were the greatest generation at that time. But today, Rumsfeld said, "This is the greatest generation." It made me feel good to hear the truth spreading.

GREAT WARRIORS KNEW THE BATTLE WAS NOT OVER

U.S. General George C. Marshall -heralded as America's foremost soldier during World War II- said in words emblazoned in the marble walls of the new WWII Memorial:

WE MUST CONTINUE TO FIGHT TO THE END;
UNTIL WE COMPLETELY DESTROY
AND TOTALLY ANNIHILATE
ALL OF OUR ENEMIES;
THEN WE WILL HAVE PEACE AT LAST

As I stood at memorial in Washington D.C. and read the General's words, I felt like I was reading my own words. It was in complete agreement with everything I had come to Washington for. The "END" has not yet come, but it is rapidly closing in upon us. It is the end of this age. It is the war that will end all wars because our enemies will not survive to ever engage in another conflict; they will be completely destroyed and totally annihilated. It is the end of war altogether, and the beginning of a period of world peace that will last for a thousand years.

As conflict wound down in Germany, U.S. General George Patton wanted to continue liberating Eastern Europe from Russian occupation. Patton warned that if you don't fight them now, you will have to fight them later.

He had a war-seasoned army already equipped and mobilized. He felt there could not be a better time to deal with this problem that he knew was not going to go away. But he was not allowed to continue.

U.S. General Douglas McArthur was prepared to take on the Chinese during the Korean War. With more than a million men, the Chinese Army came marching to the aid of the North Koreans. He knew that confrontation with China would come sooner or later. He felt it best to deal with this problem right now, or it will only grow and become worse given more time. He was told to back off, but he insisted he was right. McArthur's defiance drew the wrath of President Harry Truman who fired him. And now we've seen our tensions with China continue to intensify. Passing of time has only allowed the problem to escalate. China's official position regarding the independence of Taiwan has been stated: they will go to any length to keep Taiwan from becoming independent even if it means nuclear war with the United States.

Now we know McArthur was right when he said: "If we don't fight them now, we'll have to fight them later." But now China is a world power with nuclear weapons. They are a rapidly emerging industrial power with the young male population now estimated at approximately 130 million

Patton and McArthur were both right and the later that they spoke of is now!

CHAPTER 17

WASHINGTON D.C. AGAIN

I visited Washington, D.C., for the second time to spread the warning that the sudden destruction, the day of the Lord is coming upon America. On May 2, 2004, the Lord revealed to me another example of things to come.

I had been throughout the city of Washington D. C. all week long putting forth every effort to be heard. My mission was nearly over as I was scheduled to depart the next day. But in the middle of the last night in my room at the Omni-Shoreham Hotel, I suddenly awakened. I felt totally alert as a strange stillness permeated the room. I turned on a lamp, wondering what could have awakened me. Without being the least bit sleepy I decided to see if the Lord might be trying to tell me something.

I picked up the Bible in my hotel room and opened it. I looked at the title on the top of the page. It was the Book of Esther, and I decided to read it, as I couldn't remember the last time that I had read it.

Esther is about a good man named Mordecai and a wicked man named Haman who holds a powerful position in the kingdom. Mordecai refuses to bow down to Haman when he passes by, so Haman hates Mordecai so much that he plans to kill not only him, but also his entire race of people. Haman has the king issue a decree, an order to kill all of Mordecai's people. Haman sought to annihilate all the Jews, young and old—men, women, and children on a single day. Haman has gallows built seventy-five feet high intending to have Mordecai hung on them.

The king ordered the decree to destroy, kill, and annihilate all the Jews—young and old, women and little children—on a single day. The decree was written in 127 different languages and distributed throughout the whole kingdom spanning from Cush or the Ethiopia area of Eastern Africa to India. It was carried on specially bred horses specifically bred for the king. Today, this expanse of territory encompasses the nations primarily of the Islamic faith.

MY EFFORTS RESEMBLED THAT OF MORDECAI

When Mordecai learned of the decree against him and his people, he tore his clothes and put on sackcloth. Then, he went out into the capitol city Susa, wailing loudly and bitterly. He attempted to go to the king's palace, but he only got as far as the king's gate where he was stopped by the guards at the gate. Mordecai told the guard everything that had happened to him and gave him a written copy of the decree.

I became overwhelmed and excited as I read, because I, like Mordecai, had just gone throughout our capitol city Washington D. C. telling everyone about the plans to destroy and kill Americans on a single day (the Day of the Lord). I stood in the marble-lined halls of the United States Senate by the door to the Committee on Intelligence and wept while trying to convince the Capitol Police that I knew what was going to happen.

I even drove my rental car right up to the entrance gate to the White House (like the king's palace) where I too- like Mordecai- was stopped by the guard at the gate. The identification badge with his name on it said he was from Carson City. He asked me to state my name and where I was from. When I told him I was from the small town in Nevada, he knew where it was, not too far from his hometown. After telling him everything that had happened to me, I gave him a copy of the scriptures describing this coming attack.

Now after running around for several days all over and having experienced all these things in the capitol city of

Washington D. C., I find myself in my hotel room in the middle of the night, reading about a man with a similar story.

God is so wonderful. I cannot understand how He does these things.

For the most part, Washington, D.C., refused to listen to me. For about a week I walked in and out of Senators offices on Capitol Hill, through fish markets, the State Department, the Pentagon, a big mall and even the subways to pass out pamphlets filed with scriptures.

My frustration grew in the subway, where I heard officials announce over loudspeakers that "If you see anyone doing this, report them to authorities."

To me, it seemed almost as if authorities were aware of me. They were doing anything possible to prevent the people from learning the truth. I learned that our freedom of speech is being robbed from us by authorities afraid of letting people know the truth. In that sense, we are not a free country anymore.

HAMAN PLANNED TO HANG MORDECAI

Because Mordecai defeated Haman and refused to bow down to him, Haman ordered the construction of a seventy-five foot-high gallows—about ten stories tall for the purpose of hanging Mordecai. Imagine the considerable expense and effort to build such a massive framework to hang a single man.

Yet after it was built, Queen Esther exposed Haman as a wicked man. The king ordered Haman to be hung from those same gallows, and his people carried out the order.

Haman suffered the very fate that he had intended for his enemy Mordecai.

As I read on I recognized this is definitely another story providing us with insight of the future. Although the plans are being formed to destroy us, our enemies will die in the same way they intended for us to die. The Lord will strike the bow from their right hand and the arrows from their left. They will fall on the mountains of Israel (America), and their bodies will be food for the birds and wild animals in Ezekiel 38-39. And then the Lord will send upon their sturdy warriors a wasting disease, (radiation sickness) after they plunder the blown-up cities full of lingering radiation in Isaiah10. And the large and mighty army of Joel chapter 1 is the northern army that gets driven out in chapter 2. These are all stories that depict prophetically the same future coming conflict.

The king ordered the royal secretaries to write out a new decree according to the words of Mordecai. He sealed it with his signet ring.

Mordecai's words stated that the Jews shall have the right to assemble, (a far-reaching concept at that time) the right to protect themselves, and to totally annihilate any nation that forms armies against them which might attack men, women and children.

You can immediately see that these words are applicable to us today. After all we have the some of the same words in our Bill of Rights today. Our founding forefathers gleaned them from these scriptures.

Sealed with the king's signet, the decree was issued throughout 127 provinces stretching from India to upper Ethiopia—lands that now are occupied primarily by people of Islamic faith.

Esther 9:5 describes how the Jews struck down all their enemies with the sword, killing and destroying them. The Jews went out and slaughtered 75,000 of their enemies.

They also killed Haman's ten sons, and the fear of the Jews spread—a historical event in human history. This is interesting to note since it's exactly what the Lord says we'll ultimately do to all our enemies in the end.

There are ten kings who are represented by ten horns of the fourth beast, in Daniel's vision of four beasts. In the end, the ten kings are killed—the same thing that happened to Haman's sons.

In Ezekiel 38, the hordes of nations that come out of their places in the north have bows and arrows knocked out of their hands and they fall in a valley that will be called Hamon-Gog. Why do they call it that?

By then, it will be obvious to everyone that the story of Haman serves as an example of what has happened to our enemies.

THESE ARE SCRIPTURES FOR TODAY'S GENERATION

Esther 9:28 proclaims that *"—these days should be remembered and observed in every generation, in every province, and in every city."* The king's decree was to be remembered by their descendants and to never be forgotten. Evidently, we are the descendants of those people because the words of that decree have somehow made through thousands of years to wind up in our own Bill of Rights giving us the right to peacefully assemble.

Zachariah 2:10 proclaims that the Lord is coming, and that He will live among us; and many nations will join the Lord in that day and will become his people.

As I absorbed these details at two o'clock in the morning alone in my hotel room, I pondered their significance as it pertains toward these end-times we are facing today. I went back to sleep, but even more amazing is what happens to me the following morning.

The very next morning, I proceeded as planned to leave Washington and return home to Nevada that day. I packed my bags and checked out of my hotel, and drove my rental car down to the U.S. Capitol. I was anxious to tell someone about the truths the Lord had just revealed to me as I had read the book of Esther in the middle of the night. I intended to use every available minute to reach people before my scheduled departure by jet later that afternoon.

On the lawn in front of the Capitol, a Christian Organization had set up a temporary plywood platform with large speakers and a microphone; and they were reading the Bible non-stop, twenty-four hours a day from beginning to end, starting with Genesis and clear through Revelations. They had started at six o'clock Monday morning, and now it was Wednesday about nine o'clock in the morning. They had invited the public and government officials, including elected leaders to participate by reading a chapter of the scriptures into the microphone. They felt this was their ministry, and they had been coming to Washington D.C. to do this every year for twenty years.

I had stopped by and spoke to several of the Christians there on both Monday and Tuesday. We visited, and I told them what I was doing and gave them some of my literature.

On the two previous days that I had visited there, the event's leaders had not invited me to participate in their proceedings. But this time as soon as I arrived, a lady that I hadn't seen before came walking out toward me and asked me, "Would you like to read a chapter of the Bible?"

"I'd be delighted to," I said. She then told me to go over to the platform and stand to the side of the man now reading. When he finished I was to read the next passage.

I will never forget the moment I stepped up on the platform and heard the words the man was reading. I felt a complete tingling all over.

I immediately knew where he was reading from because I had just read those same words that morning at 2:00 am. The words he read came across the speakers clearly. The king issued the decree, and it was sent out to the 127 provinces and written in all the different languages of the people. It was sealed with the king's signet ring and sent it out to the whole kingdom by mounted couriers who rode fast horses especially bred for the king.

THIS IS THE DECREE THAT STATES THAT WE THE PEOPLE HAVE THE RIGHT ASSEMBLE, TO DEFEND OURSELVES, AND TO COMPLETELY DESTROY AND TO TOTALLY ANNIHILATE ALL OF OUR ENEMIES THAT FORM ARMIES AGAINST US.

My thoughts overwhelmed me. How is it that my very steps were timed so that when I arrived that morning, the people who had been reading the Bible continuously twenty-four hours a day for two days and nights were now in the book of Esther. And I had just woke up and read the same passage at two o'clock that same morning.

I knew it was God confirming to me that this is true—the book of Esther is another example of how this conflict at the time of the end will be fulfilled.

The moment he finished reading Chapter 8 of Esther, I took my turn and read aloud Chapter 9 to the crowd about how God's people struck down all their enemies, killing, and destroying them; and then Haman's ten sons are hung.

This is an urgent message for all of us today as we are God's people, and this is depicting the coming end-time conflict. We must now get ready and prepare for it. The Lord wants us to protect ourselves, and to kill, to completely destroy, and to totally annihilate our enemies—the same rights granted by the king. World peace will be achieved when we have no one left to fight. We are the champions of the world, but we are, only because the Lord helps us.

WE MUST PAY THE PRICE FOR PEACE

Today in Washington, D.C., the new World War II Memorial features 400 gold stars—each representing 1000 lives lost in that conflict.

The stars are at a fountain on a marble wall along with the words: **"The Price of Freedom."** I envision a future memorial for this last World War with words that say **"The Price of Peace."**

The Bible promises that a 1,000-year period of peace and prosperity will ensue after the next great conflict. Many great biblical passages reveal that slave nations headed by totalitarian governments will spark this conflict.

The people of these slave nations lack the ability to choose their leaders. But our founding forefathers established this country on the premises that the only legitimate government that exists is by the consent of the governed. Leaders in these other countries spread hatred against the United States, diverting attention from themselves. They are unwilling to have their own power taken away for they know that they cannot get the consent their people to rule over them.

Following much heartache and suffering worldwide, freedom will prevail. Rest assured that this good news shall reign for all mankind as every race, color, and creed enjoys liberty and justice. WWIII will be the "war that ends all wars."

The freedom we enjoy is under serious threat. American Revolutionary war hero Patrick Henry set an example for us when he said: "Give me liberty, or give me death." A U.S. quarter coin honoring the state of New Hampshire sums up the necessary mentality to deal with the coming troublesome times, with the phrase: "Live Free or Die."

Americans today face enemies who are willing to die for their cause. That is the measure of their commitment. If we do not become committed to the cause of freedom with an even greater commitment that our enemies how shall we prevail?

CHAPTER 18

AMERICANS WILL SURVIVE THE COMING ATTACK

In Ezekiel 38 we are told about Gog and Magog and many nations with him including Persia, Cush, and Put set out from their place in the far north (same army from the north in Jeremiah 6) to invade a land rich in goods who live in peace, and their cities have no walls. This is not the modern land we call Israel today—for that land is a land known for the violence of suicide bombers. And they are building a twenty-foot tall concrete wall forty miles long around their city in an attempt to keep out the suicide bombers.

No, but it does fit the description of our great country the United States also gathered from all the nations because people have come from all over the world to become Americans.

But after they come into our land, Ezekiel 39 says that the Lord will strike the bow from their left hand, and make their arrows drop from the right. They will fall in the open fields and become food for the wild animals.

This is similar to what Joel says about that large and mighty army that invades the land on the day of the Lord. Then that "northern army" of Joel 2:20 (the same great horde from the far north in Ezekiel 38:15, and the summoned people of the northern kingdoms in Jeremiah 1:15)—they get driven back out across the parched and barren land that they burned as they came in.

There will be so many dead men from Gog's army lying dead on the ground that it will take seven months to bury them. And the valley where they are buried will be called "Haman-Gog," because the people will then know that in the book of

Esther when Haman planned to destroy all God's people on a single day. His plans failed, and he wound up dying in the same manner he intended for God's people to die. In this end time case, it will be death from the long-term effects of nuclear bombs...radiation sickness.

Remember that in the book of Esther, Haman gets hung on the very same high gallows that he had built. He intended to hang Mordecai after his plans to annihilate all God's people on a single day. This is another example of the coming day of the Lord.

That is the same scenario also described in Isaiah 10 where we are told...woe to the Assyrian, the rod of my anger. The Lord sends him against a people who anger me (today's American society) to punish them only, but he intends to completely destroy them. As soon as he appears to be successful, he begins to boast how great he is. Therefore the Lord Almighty will send a wasting disease upon his sturdy warriors. This is the radiation sickness that they get while plundering the blown up cities. They will suffer the very fate they intended for us.

I recently had lunch with a fellow contractor who also has great concerns about the escalating hatred of America. In a very opinionated way, he told me that he thinks we should nuke every city in Iraq and turn the whole country into a sea of glass. This man is not a churchgoer, nor does he have a lot of Bible knowledge. I did not forget what he had said, but when I came home and sat down to read my Bible for a while, I read in Revelations 15, where John saw what looked like a sea of glass mixed with fire, and those who had been victorious over the beast, standing by the sea of glass were given harps. And they were singing the song of Moses,

GREAT AND MARVELOUS ARE THY WORKS
O LORD GOD ALMIGHTY, JUST AND TRUE ARE THY
WAYS
THOU KING OF SAINTS
WHO SHALL NOT FEAR THEE O LORD AND GLORIFY
THY NAME

FOR THOU ONLY ART HOLY
ALL NATIONS SHALL COME AND WORSHIP BEFORE
THEE
FOR THY JUDGEMENTS ARE MADE MANIFEST

It immediately occurred to me this is another description in the Bible of the end results of nuclear destruction and annihilation of our enemies. This sea of glass that John saw is all that is left of our enemies. Like it says in Revelations 9, one third of mankind is killed by fire, smoke, and sulfur. These scriptures confirm to me along with Zechariah 14's plague on the nations that fought against us that their flesh will rot on their bones while they stand on their feet, and their eyes will rot in their sockets, and their tongues will rot in their mouths, and a similar plague afflicts all the animals in those camps. It is complete and total nuclear annihilation of all our enemies. That is the only way there will ever be enduring world peace. Wouldn't it be great to stand victoriously by that sea of glass and join in singing the song of Moses.

A 1,000-YEAR PERIOD OF PEACE AND PROSPERITY

The Bible tells of a coming new age, the Millennial Kingdom, a 1,000-year period of continuous peace and expanding prosperity like never seen or experienced before. When war brings this present age to an end, there will be a new beginning and a time of rebuilding cities. With victory firmly established and no more threat of war ever again, men will have optimism for the future. Freedom and liberty with justice for all will be established worldwide.

It's like the example in the Book of Job; difficult times suddenly came upon him on a single day, [like the coming day of the Lord] and even though he sits in a pile of ashes [like fallout], scraping sores and boils from head to toe, with a bald head [like caused by radiation sickness] and endures a time of great personal distress, [like the coming tribulation].

Afterward, the Lord restores everything back to Job, after his trials and tribulations by giving him double what he had before. Isaiah 61:7 tells of a similar promise:

And instead of shame, "my people will receive a double portion," we shall rejoice in our inheritance, the redeemed of the Lord will return, being those who came through the fire are purified and made holy.

Isaiah proclaims the year of the Lord's favor, when he sends a messenger to bind up the broken-hearted to proclaim freedom.

Yes, Isaiah promises us the Lord shall comfort all who mourn, and provide for those who grieve. These people shall become "oaks of righteousness," purified and refined.

The people of Isaiah's visions rebuilt their ruined cities and restored places that had been attacked: "They will renew the ruined cities" that had been devastated for generations. So it will be in the days to come that the cities that suffer nuclear devastation will recover and become even greater than they were before.

FIRE, SMOKE & SULFER WILL KILL ONE THIRD OF MANKIND

Long before the advent of nuclear weapons, Zechariah 14 told that our enemies' "flesh will rot while they're standing on their feet."

Just as alarming, their eyes will rot in their sockets, and their tongues will rot in their mouths.

This is clearly the results of radiation sickness—the price they will pay for attempting to destroy America. We will execute vengeance upon them without mercy, for the judgments of the Lord are true and righteous altogether.

The Book of Ezekiel proclaims that those who refuse to listen or to heed these warnings will perish.

There are too many specific scriptures throughout the Bible that support this scenario. These verses are far too similar for us to ignore. How can so many scriptures that were written thousands of years ago just happen to perfectly describe every aspect of nuclear war as a climactic end coming? They consistently create the same example of a coming nuclear attack that does not completely destroy, but is punishment from which a recovery is made and a devastating retaliation is executed upon the enemies, completely destroying them for good.

This is the only way there will be lasting world peace, when you no longer have any enemies left to fight with.

Ultimately, we know from Revelation 19:11 that a rider on a white horse shall appear—who is called Faithful and True, our beloved savior Jesus Christ. His name is called the Word of God. With justice he judges and makes war. His eyes are a blazing fire, and his robe is dipped in blood while carrying a two-edged sword with which to strike down the nations. Guess what is following Him? He is bringing with Him "the Armies of Heaven" It is very clear to me that the second coming of the Lord Jesus Christ is quite simply a military rescue from the army of two hundred million in Revelation 9 that is closing in upon us and without this timely appearance of help from heaven we would be totally annihilated. But glory to God for He is faithful and true.

Verses 17 and 18 say *"...his vesture and thigh will be written 'KING OF KINGS AND LORD OF LORDS.' At that moment an angel shall stand in the sun, crying out to all fowls that fly in the midst of heaven to gather together to eat the flesh of kings and captains and mighty men, for the beast-the kings of the earth and their armies [of two hundred million] are gathered to make war against the rider on the white horse. They are all destroyed, and the birds are filled with their flesh."*

WHY WOULD YOU WANT TO LIVE AFTER THE ATTACKS?

Despite all the positives we know about Christ's return, people ask me: "Why would you want to live after such an attack?" This is the process referred to by Jesus as the beginning of birth pains that are necessary to produce new life. Memories of the birth pains will pass but the new life will remain forever.

And keep in mind what Isaiah 3:10 said about the righteous, *"they will survive and enjoy the fruits of their deeds,"* the Bible says.

However, this can only be accomplished by following the scriptural instructions that you've been reading.

Also, prepare to fight to the end, knowing that not everyone will survive. There's a scripture that says he who dies by the sword is better off than he who dies by famine. The sword is a quick death, but suffering the hunger pains from famine causes a slow agonizing death. So begin to immediately set aside a considerable supply of essential commodities.

ANTICIPATE INCREASED LIFE EXPECTANCY

Isaiah 65 tells us that in the coming age "he who fails to reach 100 will be considered accursed." And he who dies at a hundred will be considered a mere youth. So in the new age, under Christ's rule people will live longer, but they still grow old and die. If people are still growing old and dying, then people are also being born, and the population of the earth will continue to grow during the next thousand years.

WHAT WILL HAPPEN TO OUR GOVERNMENT?

The Bible tells us that the Lord himself is coming here to set up a new world government. Doing that is among things he'll come here to do. "Your two kingdoms will no longer be divided," is a verse that's talking about the United States and the United Kingdom.

The extreme distress of the coming war will bind together the English speaking peoples together, in their plight to survive they will become reunited, for united we stand and divided we fall.

Isaiah 9:7 says that as for the *"...increase of his government and peace, there will be no end."* And running the *"government will be upon his shoulders."*

Jesus Christ is the king of the entire world, under a single government, with liberty and justice for all.

First Thessalonians tells us that the dead will rise first, and after that we who are still alive and "remain" are caught up to meet the Lord to be with him forevermore—so that where He is, and it is here that he will be—with us—for we will still be alive, and here we will remain. {Zechariah 2:10 *"I am coming and I will live among you!"*

THE LORD ALWAYS PAYS ME BACK

In my efforts to warn the public about this message, I visited a nearby radio station; and it wanted a total $900 for twelve consecutive, once-per-week, thirty-minute pre-recorded programs.

On the spot I paid for the service in advance in cash. Five minutes later while the nine one hundred dollar bills lay spread out on the radio manager's desk, my cell phone rang.

It was the boss of an industrial plant calling to ask me if I would be their contractor, assisting them in getting a required building permit. The company intended to use their own personnel to do the work within their plant.

"How does $500 sound for your compensation?" the plant manager asked.

"How does $900 sound?" I responded.

"That's fine, Everett, we'll put the check in the mail today."

It is very obvious to me that the Lord reimburses me whenever I put out cash in an effort to spread His word.

As James 2:14 proclaims, what good is it if a man claims to have faith, but lacks good deeds?

Faith without action to back it up dies. James goes on to reiterate in 2:24 that a person is justified by the good works he does, not by faith alone. The deeds then described are tending to the physical needs of our suffering brothers and sisters who are cold and hungry.

So, start preparing, and tell as many people as you can about this message without spreading needless or senseless fear. Be sure to spread God's message of hope and fulfillment as well.

Feel free to give this document to your family and friends, or make or request copies for them. Contact me any time, for as God's faithful servant I'm eager to spread this message along with his Holy Word.

THE BIBLE AND THE LORD OF THE RINGS

The author, JRR Tolkien, was a man who spent thousands of hours studying scriptures. I see the results of his scriptural studies accurately and abundantly depicted in his trilogy, Lord of the Rings.

The gold ring represents money and the power of wealth, and the Bible states: "The love of money is the root of all evil." The ring must be destroyed is the mission.

There are rumors of the enemy forces are gathered in the dark land of mortal. North Korea as depicted by a nighttime satellite photograph is a land covered with darkness, as opposed to South Korea appearing as if lit up like a Christmas tree.

"Rise up, you men of the west," says the script. "Americans are the men of the west. The pieces all are in place, and things are now in motion that cannot be changed."

These lines of script are so appropriate for this time we are now facing. It is the time of the end. At the resounding sound of a great thunder clasp a huge whirling bolt of lightning with a flash that lights up the whole sky shoots upward followed by a piercing screech of an enormous flying dragon. It suddenly appears as hordes of troops, marching outward from the dark castle as the drawbridge gate is lowered.

Gandalf says, "It has finally come to this."

A full-fledged nuclear attack has suddenly burst forth.

Every aspect of this scene perfectly fits what I see as the Day of the Lord. It is the great thunderclap of the detonation of nuclear bombs emitting the incredibly brilliant light that will light up the sky from horizon to horizon. It has a similar affect to sheet lightning.

The bombing is followed up by the invasion of the armies of the beast.

It is the sudden attack by the beast of Revelations 13. And

the large and mighty army comes such as never was of days of old, nor ever will be in ages to come in Joel Chapter 2.

ADDITIONAL SIMILARITIES ABOUND

In "Lord of the Rings," the invading armies of orks arrived in boats and begin invading the cities. The men of the west are overrun.

The script says, "The city is lost." An ork leader stands over a wounded defender and plunges a spear down into his chest, and proclaims: "The age of man is over. The time of the ork has come."

This is depicting the end of the age that the Matthew 24 refers to and the time of the seven years of tribulation is a time the Beast will rule—lasting till the return of the Lord Jesus Christ, who is the King of Kings. This brings us to the "Return of the King," concluding author Tolkien's trilogy.

And at the end there is serenity and peace. The sun is shining, birds are singing, and flowers are blooming. Samwise, with his beautiful bride and little family, are depicting heaven on earth. This is the fulfillment of the Lord's Prayer: "Thy Kingdom Come, Thy Will Be Done, Here on Earth, as It is in Heaven."

Then, we're told: "And thus begins the fourth age of man." Well, the Fourth Age of Man is the 1,000-year millennium. The first age is the 2,000-year period from Adam to Noah. The second age is the 2,000-year period from Noah to Jesus, and the third age is the 2000 years from Jesus to the present day.

This perfectly explains Second Peter, Chapter 3, and Verse 8: *"With the Lord, a day is like 1,000 years, and 1,000 years are like a day."* Six days of work—the work being the harvest—and the harvest being the end of the age.

Another line in the script that caused me to think, "Now is the time for men to fulfill their vows." The vow that we as Americans have all taken is The Pledge of Allegiance. The day is coming when all of us who have made that pledge will be required to fulfill that vow to hold our ground, and stand and fight in the face of overwhelming odds. Those who faithfully do so will see the hand of God strike down their enemies and will see the crowds greet them with "Hail to the Victorious."

Also in "Lord of the Rings," Gollum used to be a normal hobbit. But the ring became an obsession to him, causing him to become a recluse and a wretched, miserable creature.

He murdered his friend in a struggle over the ring, which represents money and power that comes with financial influence—political control. Gollum comes to his end by perishing in the mountain volcano as he sinks out of sight in a sea of molten lava. This is a perfect depiction of Revelation 21:8, the *"...cowardly, the vile, the murderers, liars. Their place will be in the fiery lake of burning sulfur."*

In addition, the "Return of the King" Aragorn is the character depicting Jesus who is King of Kings and is going to return soon. Aragorn ventures into a dark crevice in the rock, and it's said: "No one who goes in there has ever come back out again." In there he is met by an apparition who informs him, "The Way is shut. It is kept by the dead, who suffer not the living to pass."

Jesus by his power overcame death and hell, and Aragorn's power prevails in this place as well. And Aragorn negotiates with those who are dead to come and fight with him. In the final conflict, the men are being overpowered by the armies of the beast. At the point of weakening, the tide of the battle is turned by the arrival of Aragorn leading the armies of the dead. Daniel 12 tells that the end comes when the power of the holy people is finally broken, but those who know their God will firmly resist. This is the resisting of the fourth beast that has the large teeth of iron and is devouring the whole earth—China.

Revelation 19 tells of Jesus' return as a *"...rider on a white horse whose name is called "Faithful and True, with Justice he judges and makes war."* The armies of heaven are following him. The second coming of the Lord Jesus Christ is clearly a military rescue.

Ezekiel 37 describes an army that resurrects in a valley covered with a great many bones that were very dry. And the Lord makes breath enter into them, and they come to life with a great rattling sound. And breath breathed into these slain, and they came to life and stood upon their feet—the Army of the Dead.

These bones of those who were dead are obviously resurrected. Revelation 20 describes the First Resurrection, souls who gave their lives for the blood of the Lamb and the word of their testimony, came to life and reign with Christ 1,000 years. The rest of the dead do not come to life till the 1,000 years are over.

WE NEED TO BE SAVED FROM OUR ENEMIES

Today, if you ask most people "what did Jesus come to save us from?" they will say "from our sins" and that is true, but it is a little know fact that Jesus not only came to save us from our sins but the Bible also says in Luke chapter 1 that he would save us from our enemies.

The second coming of Jesus is to save us from our enemies!

Luke 1:69-79 (New International Version)

69He has raised up a horn[a] of salvation for us

in the house of his servant David

70(as he said through his holy prophets of long ago),

71**salvation from our enemies**

and from the hand of all who hate us—

72to show mercy to our fathers

and to remember his holy covenant,

73the oath he swore to our father Abraham:

74to **rescue us from the hand of our enemies**,

and to enable us to serve him without fear

75in holiness and righteousness before him all our days.

76And you, my child, will be called a prophet of the Most High;

for you will go on before the Lord to prepare the way for him,

77to give his people the knowledge of salvation

through the forgiveness of their sins,

78because of the tender mercy of our God,

by which the rising sun will come to us from heaven

79to shine on those living in darkness
and in the shadow of death,
to guide our feet into **the path of peace.**"

Jesus coming will literally be to save the world from those who oppose Christianity and freedom, making war and prevailing. Were he to not return at this time worldwide dominance would become firmly established by our enemies. And free men would never again be able to organize and form a rebellion powerful enough to reestablish freedom and liberty.

The future of liberty and freedom is literally at stake for all generations to come.

POPULAR SONGS TELL OF THE TIMES

The song "Bad Moon Rising" by the legendary 1970s rock band Credence Clearwater Revival accurately depicts many aspects of the Day of the Lord. One line says: "I know the end is coming soon." The new moon is a sign of when this disaster is coming.

Another says: "I hear voices of rage and ruin; I see earthquakes and lightning."

The voices of rage and ruin are the sound of invading armies clashing. And earthquakes and lightning are resulting from detonating nuclear bombs.

The song says: "I hope you've got your things together; I hope you're prepared to die."

We're told to be prepared for the Day of the Lord.

Ezekiel 4 tells us to have stockpiles of wheat, barley, and beans. Luke 22:36 says to have your bags packed, and money in your purse. If you don't have a sword, sell your coat and buy one. I hope you will get your things together.

When it says "I see bad times today," to me it means I see tribulation coming. And it says, "I fear rivers overflowing" and "looks like we're in for stormy weather."

Port cities are primary targets for nuclear attack, and a nuclear mushroom cloud has an internal temperature of ten million degrees. That kind of heat will vaporize unprecedented volumes of water, forming clouds that wind currents will carry toward the mountains.

Those vaporized clouds of water can potentially cause massive cloudbursts exceeding anything rivaled by Mother Nature. I fear rivers overflowing at this time of the year when mountain reservoirs are near full capacity from the spring runoff. The normal thing to do is to hold back as much water as possible to use throughout the coming hot and drier months of summer for irrigation of crops. This will be the worst time for a huge flash flood will find the reservoirs without the ability to handle it. The potential for more water than spillways to handle could cause some reservoirs to fail and release all their water along with the greatest flashflood waters ever seen. So you can see why I fear rivers overflowing.

In addition, the song says: "Don't go out tonight; well it's bound to take your life."

Typically when people go out they go out at night, they go to the city, and cities are going to burn. It's going to be a night attack, and you're better off staying safe at home.

Now, the song's title "Bad Moon Rising" fits the scenario of Hosea 5:7, where it says a "new moon will devour them along with their fields." The fields are devoured is the same as Joel 1:11...harvest of the field is destroyed, and Joel makes it very clear that he is foretelling of the Day of the Lord. A new moon begins a cycle every month, progressing from a small crescent in the evening sky in the west to the full moon rising in the east in the early evening sky. But this moon will be a bad one.

MESSAGES IN OTHER SONGS AS WELL

Another song referring to this end-time returning of the Lord is the song titled "Seven Seas of Rhye" by the band Queen. The lyrics include lines like "I descend upon your earth from the skies to claim what is mine."

The Lord returns to claim the world that belongs to him, and the seven seas of the world are the international waters.

When the Lord comes, He announces that the kingdoms of this world are now the kingdoms of our Lord and He shall rule and reign forevermore.

The lyrics also say that he challenges the mighty titan and his troubadours. I see this as the army of 200 million in Revelation 9. They also are described in Daniel Chapter 7 as "the fourth beast" that is terrifying and frightening and very powerful. It crushes and devours the whole earth.

But when the Lord descends in Chapter 19 of Revelation, he leads the Armies of Heaven with "justice he judges and makes war. And out of his mouth comes a sharp sword with which to strike down the nations."

It fits the scriptural descriptions of what is to come.

Another song by the band Queen, titled "We Are the Champions of the World" could not be making a truer statement about the United States and England for it is the destiny of the saints—Christian/English-speaking peoples to rule and reign with the Lord when he returns.

When engaged in this final conflict we must be prepared to do as that song says, "Keep on fighting to the end" and there's "no time for losers." The song's writer says he sees it as a challenge being made for the future of the whole human race, and we are not going to lose. That is exactly the same way I see it.

The words spoken by General G. C. Marshall on the wall of the new WWII memorial just finished in Washington D.C. bear repeating.

He said, "We must continue fighting until the end, until we completely destroy and totally annihilate all our enemies, then we will have peace at last." There will be no lasting peace until they are completely destroyed.

I recognize the description of their destruction in Revelations 9 after we are told that the number of their troops is two hundred million. There are few countries today with the capacity to train, equip, and mobilize that number of troops. Then by the three plagues of fire smoke and sulfur a third of mankind is killed. That is two plus billion people.

Who is it that is being killed and who is doing the killing? We comprise only about 5% of the earth's population, so we are not who it is telling about. That is the complete destruction and total nuclear annihilation of all our enemies by us. And then we will begin the one thousand years of peace on a New Earth and never again will they train for war as in Isaiah 2.

Another song by Credence Clearwater Revival mentions "two hundred million guns are loaded, Satan cries for shame", and "...the people who know my wisdom fill the land with smoke," and that is the smoke of the three plagues of fire smoke and sulfur, that kill a third of mankind.

The movie "300" about 300 Spartans who stand off 10,000 Persians is a historic event that is a good example of how history is going to be repeated. Just substitute Greeks (Spartans are from Greece) for Americans and you have a good idea of the things to come. Daniel's vision in chapter 8 of the ram and the goat is at the of the end. The goat is the king of Greece. The two-horned ram represents the kings of Media, and Persia. Substitute the Medes and the Persians for the enemies of America today. Here the Bible is representing The United States as the kingdom of Greece. The Spartans are prepared to die to defend freedom. The New Hampshire quarter dollar has "Live free or Die" on it.

How many legitimate governments exist today? Our founding forefathers established the government of this most successful of all nations in the history of mankind on this premise: **"no government legitimately exists without the consent of the governed."** That means that only the governments of the people, by the people and for the people have the right to exist. If you believe that as deeply as I do, then we should pledge ourselves to the task of ridding the world of all illegitimate governments. These illegitimate governments do not have the right to exist without the consent of their people. The people of those governments are in fact slaves. Who will set them free? Jesus will, He sets the captives free and we will be His instruments. How will they be set free? It is by WORLD WAR THREE, the final conflict, the war that ends all wars. Let freedom ring loud and clear for a thousand years.

An end is coming. It is an end to war because it is the war that ends all wars by completely destroying all of our enemies. It is an end for them. According to Isaiah 2 men will no longer train for war, and nation will not rise up against nation any more. That is peace on earth also.

Swords will be beat into plowshares and spears into pruning hooks. This is WWWIII military surplus equipment recycled into implements of agriculture.

An end is coming. It is the end to world hunger. Mankind will no longer be consumed with weapons of war, and the tax burden of the present annual military budget of over 400 billion dollars will not be needed.

When the taxes are reduced, the economy surges forward. The best days are yet to come!

PEOPLE'S LIVES CAN BE CHANGED

The www.biblically.com is a website that I've created in an attempt to save people's lives by informing them to prepare for what is to come. The better informed you are the more prepared you can become. We do have a hope for the future. We can and will survive to see it. A world with no more war and continuing prosperity of ever expanding magnitude in part because we will no longer bear the burden of military budgets. Technology and knowledge in every field will continue to grow. Life on earth will be as in the Lord's Prayer—Thy kingdom has come and thy will is being done here on earth as it is in heaven. As it is in Heaven, so it will be here on earth in the days to come.

Until the time comes, I will continue doing whatever is possible to convey this message. If you've just read this for the first time, keep in mind that I encourage you to review it several times, and to share it with your loved ones.

Just as important, you can tell the officials or members of your church, plus various top elected leaders including local law enforcement officials to those who are making decisions on how to spend homeland defense funds and even President George W. Bush.

If you can, convey this message in an alarming, but peaceful, non-threatening manner to grab people's attention. The more people we reach before the sudden Day of the Lord, the unique disaster, the more people can prepare to deal with it.

We have a destiny to fulfill. It is to recover from this coming nuclear attack and to retaliate and completely and totally destroy all of our enemies once and for all; to usher in the new age and give to our descendants' world peace for a thousand years to come.

That is exactly what it says that the glory of the saints is, in the New International Version of Psalms 149:7-9. It is to inflict vengeance on the nations and punishment on the peoples, to bind their kings with fetters, their nobles with shackles of iron, to carry out the sentence written against them. **THIS IS THE GLORY OF ALL HIS SAINTS**. Praise the Lord. GLORY, I have seen the glory of the coming of the Lord.

He is trampling out the vintage where the grapes of wrath are stored.

GLORY, GLORY, HALLELUJAH
GLORY, GLORY, HALLELUJAH
HIS TRUTH IS MARCHING ON
COME QUICKLY LORD JESUS

THE END
HAS COME

Go to WWW. BIBLICALLY.COM